I0210886

ENCOMIUMS

William Wordsworth is at once a poet of locality and of transcendence, both the poet in English who cared most about ordinary people and the places he knew & loved, and the writer who most turned the Anglophone poetic tradition in the direction of the philosophical & the enigmatic. This edition of Wordsworth's *Fragments*, containing the essays "Hawkshead & the Ferry" and "The Sublime & the Beautiful," makes widely available for the first time key texts that demonstrate how radically thoroughgoing Wordsworth's vision was. As edited, the volume reveals a grasp of Wordsworth that can readily range from the textual to the speculative, and in his introduction, Alan Vardy brilliantly situates a Wordsworth who, in both small things and large, continues to renovate us. This is a landmark book in the continuing full understanding of the Romantic movement and demonstrates Wordsworth's seismic impact upon it.

—Nicholas Birns
The New School, New York, author of *Theory After Theory* and *Barbarian Memory*

The first and only time that William Wordsworth's fragmentary manuscript on the sublime and the beautiful appeared in print was in the 1974 Owen & Smyser three-volume edition of Wordsworth's *Prose Works*. Those volumes have long been out of print. This edition of a remarkable manuscript & its adjacent essay on Hawkshead bring much needed attention back to one of Wordsworth's most arresting prose works on the complex relation among nature, æsthetics, and mind. Readers will find here a commanding record of a poet's capacious & developing recognition of the central motives of his writing life.

— Theresa M. Kelley
Marjorie and Lorin Tiefenthaler Professor, University of Wisconsin-Madison

Selected Other Works by
William Wordsworth

Lyrical Ballads

Poems

A Guide to the Lakes

The Excursion

Laodamia

The Prelude

William Wordsworth

FRAG MENTS

FRAG
ME

Contra Mundum Press New York · London · Melbourne

William Wordsworth

NTS

INCLUDING

Hawkshead & the Ferry

AND

The Sublime & the Beautiful

EDITED BY

RAINER J. HANSHE

INTRODUCTION BY

ALAN VARDY

TEXTS & COMMENTARIES

from *The Prose Works of William Wordsworth*
edited by W.J.B. Owen & Jane Worthington Smyser.

First Contra Mundum Press
edition 2013.

Library of Congress
Cataloguing-in-Publication Data
Wordsworth, William, 1770–1850

[Fragments.]

Fragments / William Wordsworth;
edited by Rainer J. Hanshe;
preface by Rainer J. Hanshe;
introduction by Alan Vardy.

—1st Contra Mundum Press
Edition
160 pp., 7 x 10 in.

ISBN 9781940625027

I. Wordsworth, William.
II. Title.
III. Hanshe, Rainer J.
IV. Editor.
V. Hanshe, Rainer J.
VI. Preface.
VII. Vardy, Alan.
VIII. Introduction.

2001012345

TABLE OF CONTENTS

PREFACE

WHEN INITIALLY CONCEIVED, this book, *Fragments*, was to be comprised solely of Wordsworth's incomplete text, "The Sublime & the Beautiful." Although first written in the early 1800s, that text was not discovered until 1915, sixty-five years after Wordsworth's death, after which it remained in the archive of the Wordsworth Trust, accessible only to visiting scholars. The text was finally published in 1974, over 160 years after it was written, but only as an appendix to the collected edition of Wordsworth's prose works.[1]

Originally, it seemed to us that "The Sublime & the Beautiful" was a distinct entity, and that, despite its incomplete status or fragmentary nature, it merited publication in its own right, especially considering its essentially large-scale neglect, not only in Wordsworth studies, but in æsthetics in general, for its concerns expand beyond Wordsworth's poetics, if not poetics at large, actually touching upon notions of health and ethics. As a major poet's engagement with æsthetic concerns and critical dialogue with Burke, Coleridge, Kant, Knight & others, it necessitates more wide-scale attention.

---

1. William Wordsworth, "Appendix III: [The Sublime & the Beautiful]," *The Prose Works of William Wordsworth*, Vol. II, eds W. J. B. Owen & Jane Worthington Smyser (Oxford: Clarendon Press, 1974) 349–60.

However, even amongst Wordsworthians, the essay has itself received little consideration, with only a few scholars discussing it at length.[2] This neglect is not perhaps unexpected considering the history of the text, & its position in what is now, & has been, a long out-of-print cloth edition, owned primarily by libraries and not widely accessible to avid readers.[3]

To counteract that neglect — perhaps due to the character of the text and its publication history, perhaps due to critical vogues — our aim is to rescue Wordsworth's essay from academic obscurity and an invidiously supplementary status by printing it as an affordable paperback edition, thereby stressing its value & integrity as a self-contained text.

Additionally, we hope that, perhaps sometime in the future, the remainder of the text will be discovered in some overlooked trunk of Wordsworth's, in a dell in the Lake District, or stuck to the back of another manuscript, enabling us to issue a new, complete edition. A perhaps naïve longing but then, as the development of infrared technology led to the decipherment of the Oxyrhynchus papyrus and the unveiling of long lost tragedies of Sophocles as well as works by Lucian, Parthenios, Archilochos & others, a perfectly reasonable longing at that, &

2. Cf. W.J.B. Owen, "The Sublime & the Beautiful in *The Prelude*," *Wordsworth Circle* 4 (1973) 67–86; Raimonda Modiano, "The Kantian Seduction: Wordsworth on the Sublime," *Deutsche Romantik and English Romanticism*, eds Theodore G. Gish & Sandra G. Frieden (1984) 17–26; Theresa M. Kelley, "Wordsworth, Kant, and the Romantic Sublime," *Philological Quarterly* 63 (winter 1984) 134–40. See also "Archeologies," a chapter in Kelley's *Wordsworth's Revisionary Æsthetics* (1988) 13–42, and Tim Milnes, *Knowledge and Indifference in English Romantic Prose* (2003) 97–99. To cite four significant omissions, Thomas Weiskel does not discuss the text in *The Romantic Sublime* (1974), nor does Klaus P. Mortensen in *The Time of Unrememberable Being: Wordsworth and the Sublime* (1998), nor Robert Baker in his more recent book, *The Extravagant: Crossings of Modern Poetry and Modern Philosophy* (2005), nor Philip Shaw in *The Sublime* (2005), whose primary focus, when discussing Wordsworth, is *The Prelude*.

3. An e-version of the first volume was however released earlier this year, and volumes two and three are to follow in the future. Although Rev. Alexander B. Grosart's edition of *The Prose Works of William Wordsworth* (1967) is available through Project Gutenberg, it does not contain either of the essays within our volume and therefore differs from the *Prose Works* edited by Owen & Smyser.

entirely plausible. One ever more studious and diligent researcher can often discover what others assert is long missing or gone, while the sheer act of chance can yield unexpected treasures.

In preparation for writing an introduction to this book, Alan Vardy reassessed not only the main text in question but all of the prose fragments from *An Unpublished Tour*. His research forced us to not only reconsider the status of the text, but the very texts that would comprise this book, as well as how they would be arranged. Instead of publishing "The Sublime & the Beautiful" alone, Vardy suggested that we also publish the "Hawkshead & the Ferry" section of *An Unpublished Tour* as an appendix to our edition,[4] that it was in fact necessary since the two texts are actually directly related to one another, with, according to Vardy's conjectures, the former following upon the latter. Our edition would thereby restore the arrangement of the texts as originally conceived by Wordsworth. Further, Vardy also suggested excising the Borrowdale section (a text that follows upon "Hawkshead" in the aforementioned Oxford edition) since it is not actually part of *An Unpublished Tour* and has only mistakenly been grouped with it. Owen & Smyser arranged the texts such as they did for reasons that will be explained below; in addressing them, we will explain the necessity behind our arrangement.

4. "Hawkshead & the Ferry" is Wordsworth's own title but "The Sublime & the Beautiful" was given to the text by the Wordsworth Library and sustained by Owen and Smyser. The title of our edition, *Fragments*, is not Wordsworth's, but representative of the character of the texts. The former text was first published in Vol. II of *The Prose Works of William Wordsworth*, ibid., 321–40.

Operating on a generic basis, when editing their edition of Wordsworth's prose works, Owen and Smyser separated the proto-guidebook material from the philosophical fragment, "The Sublime & the Beautiful," & placed it in an appendix. Their editorial decision to end *An Unpublished Tour* with the Borrowdale section was based on the evolution of those texts into the *Guide through the Lakes*. However, as they themselves carefully explain, the Borrowdale section is a different manuscript altogether: it appears in an *Excursion* notebook of Wordsworth's, and could have been written as early as 1806, whereas the remainder of the *Unpublished Tour* manuscript, including "The Sublime & the Beautiful," dates to 1811.[5] The rest of the manuscript, including "Hawkshead & the Ferry" and "The Sublime & the Beautiful," are all-of-a-piece, which is evident upon a physical examination of the texts: they're written on the same paper, with the same ink, have similar water stains, and are in Mary Wordsworth's hand. They are clearly dictations. Gordon Wordsworth, the poet's grandson, discovered the manuscript bundle, in much disarray, in a cupboard around 1915; he arranged them as best he could and made a rough transcription. He separated "The Sublime & the Beautiful" from the rest and Owen and Smyser adopted his decision.

What Vardy seeks to achieve by excising the Borrowdale section and returning the æsthetic fragment to the immediate context of "Hawkshead & the Ferry" is make its relationship to Wordsworth's actual touring explicit. "The Sublime & the Beautiful" does not emerge as a philosophical study, but rather as *a lived response* to the problem of valuing landscape and experience. Owen and Smyser conjecture that at least one manuscript sheet is lost between these two texts, implying that possibly more sheets are lost. It seems likely that it is actually just one sheet, or the equivalent of four manuscript pages, which is missing. One manuscript ends with a geographical location, with Wordsworth standing on the west side of Windermere looking north

5. See page XLII for Owen & Smyser's conjecture on the dating of these manuscripts & Wordsworth's decision to cease completing them.

to the Langdales, & the next begins in the exact same spot as Wordsworth struggles to understand his æsthetic views and commitments.

Owen and Smyser's edition & their scrupulous account of their editorial procedures made many of Vardy's conjectures possible. After discussing them with me however, I decided that instead of relegating "Hawkshead" to an appendix, considering Vardy's discoveries and his new understanding of the texts, it is more philologically accurate to begin our edition with "Hawkshead," set blanks where the missing manuscript pages would be, then follow suit with "The Sublime & the Beautiful." In this, we aim to honor the arrangement of the texts as Wordsworth himself conceived them, replicating as accurately as possible their true order.

In the future, perhaps an illustrated edition of *An Unpublished Tour,* including "The Sublime & the Beautiful," can be produced. For now, we must content ourselves with this edition whereby including "Hawkshead" provides necessary context for understanding the textual & intellectual challenges of "The Sublime & the Beautiful." May it stimulate renewed interest in Wordsworth's fragments.

Rainer J. Hanshe
October 15, 2013
Berlin

INTRODUCTION

"Let me then invite the Reader": Wordsworth on Æsthetic Sensation

IN HIS PROSE FRAGMENT "The Sublime & the Beautiful," Wordsworth invites the reader to look north "towards that cluster of Mountains at the Head of Windermere." He hopes that our gaze will naturally settle on the Langdale Pikes and that we will concur with him about their æsthetic value. The problem is how to ensure such unanimity and create a universal judgment of their sublimity or beauty. As the passage continues, the scale of the problem becomes clear as Wordsworth notes differences in æsthetic response dependent on proximity to the mountains, the specific viewer's experience of mountain scenery, and the scene's 'natural' power to produce the "sensation of sublimity." He speculates about the constituent parts in judging a scene sublime, producing more questions than answers. How do the Langdales and "their power to affect" establish our judgments of taste? How does "sensation" become judgment? The answers to these questions are not forthcoming. This prose fragment was clearly intended as a philosophical supplement to *A Guide through the Lakes* (1820; 1822; 1823; 1835). That it never found a place in that text points to Wordsworth's dissatisfaction with his formulations.

This new edition of "The Sublime & the Beautiful" seeks to rehabilitate the text by focusing not on its æsthetic failures, but rather on its struggles — recasting the interplay of sensation, æsthetic doubt, pleasure, et cetera, to offer a map (as opposed to a theory) of the sublime and the beautiful. Further, the manuscript is part of the single bundle of prose scraps discovered by Gordon Wordsworth, the poet's grandson, and this edition returns it to its original context as the final fragment in the series collectively known as *An Unpublished Tour*; specifically, we have reprinted the section "Hawkshead & the Ferry," which immediately precedes it, thus our new title: *Fragments: "Hawkshead & the Ferry" and "The Sublime & the Beautiful."* The latter text is famous for its failures. Neither readers nor Wordsworth find satisfactory answers, yet in this confusion we find the essential problems at the heart of any consideration of philosophical æsthetics: how do we manage the interplay between a natural object producing a sensation we recognize as sublime, and our subsequent internalization of that sensation as philosophical speculation? Before we address these problems, I want to situate us by imagining how we came to be standing on the west bank of Windermere looking north.

W.J.B. Owen & Jane Worthington Smyser, the editors of Wordsworth's *Prose Works*, conjecture that this perceptual moment arises from a contiguous tour, "Hawkshead & the Ferry," the penultimate section from another set of prose fragments collectively called *An Unpublished Tour*. This particular walk, like many of what we might call the proto-*Guide* fragments, is full of heterogeneous stuff — local anecdote, history, et cetera, as well as advice on the best picturesque views on route. What fascinate are the moments when these various registers overlap & interact. Early on, Wordsworth comments on the lamentable phenomenon that, in "a Country so beautifully framed & prodigiously adorned," many of the houses are turned away from the prospect. He makes a strong æsthetic inference: "though utter insensibility or absolute indifference to the general forms of Nature does not exist in any state of society, however rude — a relish for fine combinations of Landscape is assuredly an acquired taste" (6). This is partly good business, arguing as it does for the need of a guide to acquiring such taste, but it also announces the pressure on Wordsworth's project as a whole, and "The Sublime & the Beautiful" in particular, as the means by which such taste might be confirmed and secured.

The stakes are made clear in the next passage. Passing an Anabaptist chapel on the road, Wordsworth tells the tale of a member of the congregation who was "oppressed by religious melancholy" despite living "at the head of the wild valley of Langdale" (9). One day the man "rose up from the table where he had been reading his Bible & dropped some words intimating that he should be seen no more" (9). His auditors ignored him, & eventually his scattered remains were found in the hills, and interred in the burial ground where we imaginatively stand with our poet-guide. The utter lack of solace that dooms this poor man (religion seems an implicit cause of his despair) refigures slightly the stakes of the tour — could it be possible to learn to admire the beauty of the valley of Langdale, so conspicuously unavailable to this man who lived in its midst? In other words, might taste, once cultivated, prove salvatory?

That this anecdote deliberately confuses religious and æsthetic doubt is made evident in a subsequent entry occasioned by viewing the "plain marble slab sacred to the memory of Eliz.[abeth] Smith" (14) in Hawkshead Church. Smith had been a local beauty and autodidact whose extensive learning and unsuspected genius had only been discovered after her death, leading to a series of posthumous publications, including a translation of Klopstock.[1] The quality and range of her achievements, hitherto unknown, caused an outpouring of tributes (De Quincey wrote about her in one of his *Tate's* articles in the 1840s). Wordsworth emphasizes her intense attachment to natural beauty, as "a mind tenderly alive to the beautiful in every thing," and situates her in the immediate landscape: "The loftiest peaks that were accessible to female feet had been trodden by her light steps, & the deepest dells were not unknown to her" (14). Elizabeth's "light steps" suggest a tenuous link to the material world even in the midst of her presumed æsthetic raptures. Beyond its obvious pathos, the passage directly involves the reader, whom Wordsworth calls his "Companion" on the guided walking tour, by reminding us that we'd experienced the physical beauty that so moved Elizabeth Smith as we walked from Coniston to Hawkshead. In her final days, refusing to relocate to a "milder climate" for her health, she declared that, in "fixing her glistening eyes" upon the view of Coniston Water from a knoll near her father's house, that: "if she could not be well with such a heavenly sight before her, she could be well no where" (15). In this declaration, Smith serves as a guarantor of the value of

1. *Memoirs of Frederick and Margaret Klopstock* (1810).

the local landscape, momentarily eliding the doubt & æsthetic anxiety preceding it.

Hawkshead Church becomes a sort of pivot around which the gaze of Wordsworth's imagined walking party rotates. As we leave the church, "we cross the Vale on our way toward the Ferry house of Windermere" (15), and turn partly back to see the Old Man of Coniston to the west. Wordsworth rhetorically lingers over this view, producing a pious final glance at Elizabeth Smith; he hopes the view:

> ... at least soothed her pain, lifted up her spirits, & through the medium of perishable things reminded her, as by a faint reflexion, of regions maintained by the love of the Almighty in secure & undecaying beauty. (15)

Hoped-for religious solace, not certainty, characterizes this moment. The æsthetic grandeur of the timeless mountain, at least for this moment, speaks of a divinity beyond human reckoning.

From here we carry on our way, but turn a final time to bring the Langdale Pikes into view behind the "white church of Hawkshead" (16), finally losing the church as we drop out of the Vale of Esthwaite (although the Langdales remain in the background), and complete our descent down to the Ferry house at Windermere.[2] This walk then conditions the fragment on "The Sublime & the Beautiful"; our walking motion through the landscape, our looking back, pressing forward, linger-

2. Hawkshead and environs provide the focus for the walk from Coniston to Windermere (the final descent to the shore doesn't appear). Hawkshead sits in a tight valley up above both large lakes, thus turning in the landscape tends to alternately obscure and reveal. The church, situated on a hill at the apex of the walk (both figuratively and topographically), is the most constant object, even more than the Langdale Pikes. The view from Anne Tyson's house in Hawkshead, where Wordsworth boarded when he was at school, provides an example of how the landscape works. After a few years, Tyson moved to the adjacent village of Colthouse in search of more space, and took her boarders with her. Wordsworth's view every morning from the first cottage, situated below the church, was of the Langdales in the distance, but once they moved to

ing, makes any single account of our æsthetic experience impossible, even absurd. Further, we carry numerous inevitable associations in our wake: the religious melancholy of the suicide, Elizabeth Smith's beautiful suffering, and perhaps most important, the poet's childhood memories of this, his home place. Wordsworth's childhood association, he readily admits, accounts for, in his words, the fact that we have "lingered too long in a Vale of so little celebrity" (22). The singular moment of this lingering attachment is not properly part of our tour at all, but rather a childhood memory recounted by our poet-guide. Nostalgic for the wild swans that once inhabited the Vale, he paints a tableau of the picturesque beauty and accompanying associations, which constitute *his* affective response to that part of the tour. Describing his memory of the swans, he writes:

> Their towering wings & snow white plumage harmonize with the white Church of Hawkshead, standing at some distance upon the hill & leading the eye to the hoary pikes of Langdale by which the horizon is bounded. (19)

Wordsworth's æsthetic fragment on "The Sublime *&* the Beautiful" *begins* in *media res* with the closing fragment of a sentence "... amongst them" (33). The "them" are the Cumbrian mountains through which we've been touring, and Wordsworth imagines us "situated" "amongst them" and expresses his faith that we will be moved by their presence and proximity. However, uncertainty creeps into his declaration via its torturous negative formulation:

> It is not likely that a person so situated, provided his imagination be extended by other intercourse, as it ought to be, will become, by any continuance of familiarity, insensible to sublime impressions from the scenes around him. (33)

Colthouse, he awoke to the reverse shot (the cinematic conceit seems apt here) of the craggy vastness of Coniston Old Man, which dominates the view. That mountain, and its sublimity, had been habitually at his back while he lodged in Hawkshead, but became omnipresent after the move of less than two miles along the valley.

Why not simply say that familiarity will not diminish the effect of the sublime? Why are we "not likely" to be "insensible?" The conditional clause makes matters worse by confusing the "situated" experience of "sublime impressions" and philosophical reflection about such experiences. The hectoring "ought to be," instructing us to develop our imaginations after the fact, rather defeats the "situated" moment. The move from the complex experiences recorded on the walk from Hawkshead to writing about æsthetic value and judgment proves fraught. Does the syntax betray the essential difficulty of æsthetics: moving from the "sensible" experience to constructions of the philosophical status and value of that experience? The walk revealed momentary glimpses of beauty and sublimity that were inseparable from associations flooding the viewer's mind. Can we actually separate æsthetic value out from this experiential complexity?

Wordsworth tries his best, and succeeds in offering not a solution to this vexing problem, but rather an account of his struggles with it. Unsurprisingly, he begins by noting the affective power of sublimity and beauty, focusing on their emotional and psychological value. He avoids a full philosophical disquisition, stating: "Neither the immediate nor final cause of this [æsthetic experience] need here be examined" (33). Instead he inverts a common valuation of the two, asserting that neither "commonness [nor] frequency" will diminish such experiences, but this is "more strikingly felt in the influences of beauty" than "with respect to grandeur" (33). He makes the point explicitly: "though it is impossible that a mind can be in a healthy state that is not frequently and strongly moved by sublimity and beauty, it is more dependent for its daily well-being upon the love & gentleness which accompany the one, than upon the exaltation or awe which are created by the other" (33). Æsthetic theory, then as now, tends to concentrate on the sublime at the expense of the beautiful. Burke is notorious in this regard, and Kant makes matters worse as the sublime is the whole reason to formulate æsthetic judgment, given its place in the system building of the three *Critiques*. Æsthetic debates were a constant in Wordsworth's intellectual life, and he agrees with much of the philosophical consensus:

> I need not observe to persons at all conversant in the speculations that I take for granted that the same object may be both sublime & beautiful: or, speaking more accurately, that it may have the power of affecting us both with the sense of beauty & the sense of sublimity; tho' (as for such Readers I need not add) the mind cannot be affected by both these sensations at the same time, for they are not only different from, but opposite to each other. (33–34)

The absolute distinction between the two experiences holds true for the empiricist Burke and the idealist Kant. More surprising is the claim that a single object may elicit both affective responses. Although this is less surprising in the context of Wordsworth's walk from Hawkshead, in which the viewer's relationship to various mountains constantly shifted as they moved, creating ever-new experiences of various kinds. Wordsworth's double evocation of the qualified reader proves crucial, as familiarity with æsthetic speculations conditions how we see, at least after the fact. Contrasting such readers with visitors unfamiliar with "Mountainous Country," Wordsworth notes that the overwhelming sense of awe on our first experience of such sights holds true regardless of the age of the viewing subject.

At this early point, Wordsworth threatens to conclude his philosophical speculations without elaborating any further, fearing that philosophy might alienate the audience of the *Guide*. After apologizing that his discussion might prove "both tedious & uninstructive" (34), and conceding that a guidebook isn't the place for philosophical speculation, especially on a subject notorious for "the errors by which it has been clouded" (34), he nonetheless carries on with an account of the "principle laws" by which sublime and beautiful objects "everlastingly affect the mind" (34). To accomplish this goal he returns us to the western shore of Windermere, looking north to the Langdale Pikes. From this position, the Pikes form the "crown of a comprehensive Landscape," and produce what he calls a "grand impression and nothing more" (35). A "grand impression" falls short of sublimity, & Wordsworth develops his earlier claim that single objects can produce a variety of affective states, by shifting us through the landscape until we reach a position where the Langdale Pikes *are* sublime: "if they be looked at from a point which has brought us so near that the mountain is almoſt the sole objeſt of our eyes, yet not so near that the whole of it is visible, we shall be impressed with a sensation of sublimity" (35). In such a moment, the experience remains unorganized, "a sensation" which is involuntarily "impressed" upon us. The shift, then, from æsthetic experience to philosophy (the organizing of æsthetic value into a set of coherent principles) produces Wordsworth's central formulation of a 'theory' of the sublime, suggeſtively referred to as an analysis of "the body of this [sublime] sensation" (35). Sensations are by definition unorganized, & this presents a challenge for a treatise that hopes to syſtematize our underſtanding of æſthetic experience while we move through the ever-changing landscape of the tour. The sublime then becomes an arreſting event, ſtopping us in our tracks, demanding we take in the objeſt that has occasioned it.

The fragment works like a more focused version of the walk from Hawkshead, resiſting associations, honing in on the sublime event. However, in order for it to find a place in the *Guide* as a philosophical supplement, Wordsworth muſt isolate the conſtitutive parts of that event. He suggeſts three simultaneous "senses," which combined, create the sublime: "a sense of individual form or forms; a sense of duration; and a sense of power" (35); further, "the effeſt depends on their co-exiſtence" (35). Problems immediately ensue. Form alone, even the grandeur of the Langdales viewed from the right position, cannot be sublime. Why not? The answer lies in Wordsworth's anxiety that his much-valued home scenes may not always affeſt even him. Thus he claims formal grandeur muſt be "contemplated under the notion of duration," and further that the mountain muſt ſpeak to us of "the duration belonging to the Earth itself" (36). While geological time is certainly sublime, contemplation of it cannot be part of an æsthetic experience. Contemplation itself caſts the moment into the paſt. In a Kantian schema, we cease making a judgment, thus leave æsthetics behind, & entertain ideas of what makes the view good. The physical mass of the mountain may elicit awe or terror at firſt sight, but over time the scene becomes domeſticated by repetition (one of the key reasons for the initial claim that, psychologically, beauty is to be preferred to sublimity). Nonetheless, that firſt view *is* sublime:

"a Child or an unpracticed person [one who has not yet contemplated] whose mind is possessed by the sight of a lofty precipice, with its attire of hanging rocks & starting trees, &c., has been visited by a sense of sublimity, if personal fear & surprise or wonder have not been carried beyond certain bounds" (38). The language of usurpation returns here: the "mind is possessed" and "visited" by the sublime. The vacillation between the sensational and the contemplative makes the exposition of the treatise difficult to follow here let alone evaluate. Theresa Kelley notes the problem of the child's response in relation to "duration": "Because a child's sensation of sublimity is likely to be too caught up in 'awe or personal apprehension,' few children are likely to recognize an idea of duration in their experience of the sublime."[3] Quite, and in hoping to preserve the sublime as possible even in cases of repeated viewings of the identical scene, Wordsworth inadvertently introduces personal need into his system. To imagine perception of physical mass as simultaneous with perception of the duration of that mass ignores an unavoidable temporal interval from one to the other. The child reveals the folly of the formulation.

The essential confusion in Wordsworth's exposition of key terms is made worse by a crucial deletion he made to the text. His original manuscript reveals a stark instance of how these formulations are a casting about for certainty. When the reader reaches the famous passage formulating the "three senses" which are simultaneously necessary for the sublime, they discover the word "three" above the crossed-out word "four," and a deletion of an abandoned fourth "sense." I want to stop a minute to restore this deletion: "The sense of motion, abrupt, rapid or precipitous as expressed by the outlines of the mountains before us" (35). This "sense," removed from the philosophical schema, most closely describes our æsthetic experiences on the road from Hawkshead. 

3. Kelley, *Wordsworth's Revisionary Æsthetics* (1988) 26–27. Kelley's chapter "Archeologies" remains the most comprehensive discussion of "The Sublime & the Beautiful." In it, she differentiates Wordsworth's æsthetic formulations from Burke's, and is particularly interested in Wordsworth's intention to focus most strongly on the beautiful — an unfulfilled expectation. See Kelley, ibid., 13–42.

4 3

~~making us conscious of its presence This is so strikingly true with respect to the forms of Nature that the qualities of beauty will almost be entirely overlooked by a spectator where they are involved in a sublime object with which he may be unfamiliar.~~

As I do not wish to weary the Reader with dry & abstract spe-
culations ~~I will at once refer to a mountainous country, as into such we are about to enter, in illustration of my notions of the sublime as it exists in landscape.~~ Let us
~~turn our eyes together towards that cluster of mountains at the head of Windermere they it is probable that they will settle~~
long upon the Pikes of Langdale & the black precipice
contiguous to them. If these objects be so distant, that while
we look at them they are only thought of as the crown of
a comprehensive Landscape if our minds be not perverted
by false theories unless those mountains be seen under
some accidents of nature we shall ~~[illegible]~~ receive from them
a grand impression and nothing more but if they be looked
at from a point which has brought us so near that the mountain is almost the sole object before our eyes yet not so
near but that the whole of it is visible ~~if this be analyzed~~
we shall be impressed with a sensation of sublimity. and if this
~~if~~ analyzed the body of this sensation ~~will~~ would be found to resolve
itself into ~~four~~ three component parts — a sense of individual form
or forms ~~of motion~~, abrupt, ~~rapid or precipitous~~ ~~[illegible]~~
~~by the outlines of the mountain before us~~ — a sense of

Wordsworth Library MSS Prose 28b, folio 3 recto.

We started with the kinetic experience of sublime and beautiful objects coming into view as we were in transit through the landscape. The various views of the Langdales unfolded as we looked back, turned, looked back again. Our current position on the western shore of Windermere looking north at the mountains bounding our view produces grandeur, but movement toward them brings them into active engagement with the mind, an engagement that is too "rapid" & variegated to control — thus sublime. The deletion of the "sense of motion" is necessary to the system-building needs of his argument. "Form" becomes fluid as our relation to stationary objects shifts, as Wordsworth demonstrated at the outset by moving to different positions vis-à-vis the mountain. Contemplating "duration" requires cessation of movement, both of the feet and the mind. In short, there is no way to incorporate "motion" into his idea of the necessary co-existence of "form," "duration," & "power," in producing the sublime "effect."

Wordsworth imports Coleridge's ideas for conceptual help and an air of authority: "For whatever suspends the comparing power of the mind & possesses it with a feeling or image of intense unity, without a conscious contemplation of parts, has produced that state of the mind which is the consummation of the sublime" (38). Coleridgean suspension restores the intensity of the lived moment, & rescues the formulation, briefly, from "contemplation" and the loss of the affective power occasioning the treatise in the first place. Wordsworth received his Kantian orientation via Coleridge's active engagement with the philosopher, & in this textual moment that 'training' allows him a subtle negotiation of the problem as it unfolds.

The other obvious influence that develops Wordsworth's thinking is Richard Payne Knight's *Analytical Inquiry*. He and Coleridge had discussed and annotated a copy as early as circa 1806, and no later than their quarrel in 1810.[4] The formal divisions of Knight's treatise tell the tale. Part I, "Of Sensation," offers a detailed account of the effect of æsthetic objects on the various "organs of sense." Part II, "Of the

4. Kelley, ibid., 218, note 53.

Association of Ideas," begins with a section called "Of Knowledge, or Improved Perception."[5] The first proposition in this section concerns the marked difference between unorganized sensation and perception, the latter implying reflection, however brief, on the prior sensation. "Improved perception" implies that repetition over time & subsequent reflection produce the æsthetic judgements that we associate with taste. This idea speaks to Wordsworth's crisis at the outset: how to secure the æsthetic value of the Langdale Pikes despite the disparate nature of possible views and habituation with even the most sublime prospects? Knight's solution was to embrace the inevitability of change, and instead of mourning the loss of affective power, to celebrate the processes by which we make associations after the fact — the turn back toward Hawkshead Church, & the inevitable associations of childhood, the swans, & Elizabeth Smith. The title "Of the Association of Ideas" places Knight's æsthetic theory neatly into a comprehensive associationist psychology. Knight was worthy of their scrutiny, & offered Wordsworth at least a possible solution to his crises of æsthetic experience: the waning of pleasure, the loss of affect. Predictably, however, their marginalia consists of disagreements with Knight over the status of specific associations. Claims of universal value based on association can always be picked apart & revealed as personal biases. For example, the poets dismiss Knight's critique of Burke's understanding of the difference between actual physical privation and its personification in literature. They argue, for example, that "the sensation of thirst is a sufficient cause in the production of the sublime as it calls forth the modifying power of the Imagination."[6] "Imagination" in Knight refers to the mental processes by which we make associations, so their objection is to the author confusing his own terms — the sensation of thirst is always

5. Richard Payne Knight, *An Analytical Inquiry into the Principles of Taste* (1805) 94–131.

6. Edna Aston Shearer & Julian Ira Lindsay, "Wordsworth and Coleridge Marginalia in a Copy of Richard Payne Knight's *Analytical Inquiry into the Principles of Taste*," *Huntington Library Quarterly* I (October 1937) 71.

convertible into the sublime via the "improved perception" of imaginative reflection. Inevitably, the same charge they make against Knight can be brought against any of Wordsworth's associations — the impossibility of the sense of "duration" occurring simultaneously with the sense of power, for example, undermines the philosophical treatise, while his love for the swans can finally only be personal.

The rest of the fragment drifts toward a Kantian position, culminating in the declaration: "[t]o talk of an object being sublime or beautiful in itself, without references to some subject by whom that sublimity or beauty is perceived, is absurd" (42). The Kantian drift begins with a growing confidence in the narrating voice.[7] A single manuscript page demonstrates the turn toward expressions of æsthetic certainty.[8] Folio 12, verso of MS *Prose* 28^{b}, contains a series of deletions and immediate replacements on the same line, clearly indicating the process of dictation. As such, they offer a glimpse of Wordsworth's thinking as it develops. He strikes "has impressed" & then "should be thought of as having" in favor of "our sympathy impresses" removing all qualification & proceeding in a confident present tense. He next strikes "might seem that the notion of resistance implies" in favor of "implies a two-fold agency," and then simply strikes the qualification:

7. I say "narrating" because it is clear in the manuscripts that Wordsworth is dictating to his wife Mary, who serves as amanuensis. Owen's note that there appear to be three drafts of the fragment is somewhat misleading. There is a single manuscript with emendations indicating that there were two sets of revisions. However, the ink is identical throughout and there is no reason to think that the compositional process — eventually abandoned — lasted more than a few weeks. The paper, ink, and hand for "The Sublime & the Beautiful" and *An Unpublished Tour* are identical, thus Owen's conjecture that they 'might' be contiguous is clearly understated. If the fragment immediately follows the tour, then it is reasonable to conjecture that no more than a single leaf (two sheets, four recto and verso pages) is lost, as Wordsworth quickly conducts the reader to the shore of Windermere where we ended the previous segment of our tour. Similarly, Owen's internal conjecture date of 1811 based on the incorporation of the second Duddon tour into *An Unpublished Tour* is bolstered by the use of the word "Luddites" to describe illiterate rural insurrectionists, a word reliably dateable to 1811. In addition, the "Hawkshead & the Ferry" section cannot be earlier than 1807, as Elizabeth Smith's commissioned marble memorial in the church records the date

"It therefore appears that in which."[9] The resulting text removes verbal and intellectual uncertainty by doing away with equivocation. The effect on the manuscript page is stark, as there are otherwise no emendations; it reads as Wordsworth gaining his stride. In enumerating the effects of "power," he presents "that mighty mass of Waters" (41) of the waterfall at Chafhausen on the Rhine, & describes the cognitive processes by which they enter the mind as sublime:

> ... there are undoubtedly here before us two distinct images & thoughts; and there is a most complex instrumentality acting upon the senses, such as the roar of the Water, the fury of the foam, &c.; and an instrumentality still more comprehensive, furnished by the imagination, & drawn from the length of the River's course, the Mountains from which it rises, the various countries thro' which it flows, & the distant Seas in which its waters are lost. (41–2)

The drift from the phenomenal to the abstract, as the imagination removes us from the perceptual moment and into contemplation, feels like usurpation — the "instrumentality" of the object acting on the mind superseded by "an instrumentality" "more comprehensive." He moves another step toward abstraction with: "These images & thoughts will, in such a place, be present to the mind, either personally or by representative abstractions more or less vivid" (42). "More or less"? Again, this is the fundamental tangle of the treatise: how to remain present

of her death as August 7, 1806. Further, the paper stock has a legible watermark of 1806; thus, the MS is reliably dated to no earlier than 1807 and no later than 1811. That being the case, the whole should be understood as initial, perhaps preliminary, forays into the guidebook genre — a project suspended in 1813 with the welcome arrival of income from his new position as commissioner of stamps for Westmoreland.

8. Raimonda Modiano described this movement as the "Kantian seduction" in her 1981 conference paper, "The Kantian Seduction: Wordsworth on the Sublime," discussed in Kelley (216, n. 32).

9. Wordsworth Library MSS Prose 28^b, folio 12 verso. S&B, 41.

"in such a place" while constructing the sublime as a retrospective event based on complex intellectual associations? Wordsworth returns us to "the rock & the Waterfall" and admits that "these objects will be found to have exalted the mind to the highest state of sublimity," yet he cannot leave well enough alone and remain in the experience, but draws an analogy with the effect on the mind of conceiving of "parallel lines in mathematics, which, being infinitely prolonged, can never come nearer to each other" (42). The analogy points to a desire to plot the impossible, as if we might write an algorithm for the sublime and secure æsthetic value by abstraction and a kind of translation. The underlying emotional and psychological strain seem palpable here, and reminiscent of that moment in Book X of *The Prelude* when, wearied from attempting to make sense of the social and political chaos subsuming him, he:

> Yielded up moral questions in despair,
> And for [his] future studies, as the sole
> Employment of the enquiring faculty,
> Turned towards mathematics, and their clear
> And solid evidence.[10]

The mess of everyday existence effaced by abstract certainty appeals, and the effort after æsthetic judgment follows the same path. The text ultimately drifts toward overstatement: "nor is it of the slightest importance whether there be any object with which their minds are conversant that Men would universally agree ... to denominate sublime or beautiful" (42). An excellent point about the common mistake of thinking that subjective universality means we all agree in our æsthetic judgment of any single object,[11] is marred by the phrase "nor is it of any impor-

10. *The Prelude* (1805) Book X, ll. 900–4.

11. Indeed, this mistake in reading Kant is distressingly common, usually as a prelude to denouncing his æsthetics as elitist. Subjective universality, as Wordsworth knows, suggests that each human subject undergoes the same cognitive processes when confronted by an æsthetic experience.

tance," which has the effect of denigrating the physical scene and our apprehension of it. The hectoring tone here seems odd, almost absurd, given that we are in a *Guide through the Lakes*, not through the mind. It is as if, performatively, we — Wordsworth's walking companions/readers — are blamed for being overly fixated on the mighty river (or the Langdales), even though he has 'conducted' us to the view & 'fixed' our gaze there. The tone is only disrupted by a lost sheet in the manuscript:[12]

> The true province of the philosopher is not to grope about in the external world & ... to set himself the task of persuading the world that such [an object] is a sublime or beautiful object, but to look into his own mind & determine the law by which it is affected. (42–3)

I had been enjoying "groping about" on the road from Coniston to Hawkshead; almost the final word before the accidental gap in the argument is the dismissive "ludicrous" — to have affection for physical objects has now become almost beneath contempt.

The lost folios 15 and 16 then disrupt the growing confidence of producing a treatise. The fragment following the gap affects a grandeur suitable to its subject, if unrecoverable: "... to power as governed some where by the intelligence of law & reason, and lastly to the transcendent sympathies which have vouchsafed to her [power] with the calmness of eternity" (43). The rest of his disquisition on "power" can only be guessed at. The composed tone is in stark contrast with the hectoring Kantianism at the other end of the gap. The sense of equipoise resounds in what appears to be the concluding paragraph in exposition: "Thus, then, is apparent how various are the <u>means</u> by which we are conducted to the same end — the elevation of our being; & the practical influences to be drawn from this are most important, but I shall consider them only with reference to the forms of nature which have occasioned this disquisition" (43). The overlay of registers here speaks volumes about the central conundrum with which he wrestles. In the

12. It would have been numbered folios 15 & 16.

classic formulation of the guidebook, "we are conducted," not to a specific physical view, but rather to the universalizable "same end." Our mountain scenery becomes interiority — "the elevation of our being." This may seem to be the end of Wordsworth's Kantian move, but an abrupt swerve surprises us and we discover ourselves back where we started, by the side of Windermere looking north at the Langdales, "the forms of nature which have occasioned" all that has come before. By the time we reach the 'end,' Wordsworth's Kantian self-confidence has dissipated. As he prepares to turn to the beautiful as promised at the outset, he shares a final warning against being seduced by theories of the sublime:

> I cannot pass from the sublime without guarding the ingenuous reader against those caprices of vanity & presumption derived from false teachers in the philosophy of the fine arts & of taste, which Painters, connesieurs, & amateurs are perpetually interposing between the light of nature & their own minds. (46)

So the ultimate risk is that any theory of the sublime may simply create an artificial barrier between the perceiving subject and æsthetic experience. It would be difficult to conceive of a more compelling reason to abandon a piece of writing. The emphasis on beauty that promised to differentiate Wordsworth's æsthetics from those of his close contemporaries never appears, and it is clear from the manuscript that this was a conscious choice, not another accidental elision.

While the confusions in Wordsworth's fragment may seem like further instances of the problems of reconciling empirical & idealist accounts of æsthetic experience, it might be productive to begin again with "sensation" and consider how such experiences lead inevitably to associations after the fact, which in turn condition our future evaluation of those experiences. The walk from Hawkshead created such a set of associations: the turn back toward Hawkshead Church, the inevitable associations of childhood, Elizabeth Smith, etc. The impossibility of reaching consensus on the status or value of personal associations makes æsthetic arguments vexing. Such vexations, however, in our current critical moment with its fascination with phenomenology, affect, sensation — the stuff from which philosophy emerges — indicate that Wordsworth's confusions and contradictions, rather than marking simple failures, provide productive sites in which we glimpse the inevitable vacillation between the value of immediate experience and the future abstractions it engenders.

That this fragment was to have found its place in a longer *Guide through the Lakes* seems clear enough. Had it been successful, it would have established a universal basis by which the various 'beauty spots' of a tour might be valued. Remember that the various manuscripts that eventually became *A Guide through the Lakes* began as an entrepreneurial venture; a paid supplement for Joseph Wilkinson's series of engravings, *Select Views in Cumberland, Westmoreland, and Lancashire* (1810). *An Unpublished Tour* was written as the beginnings of an independent effort to produce a guide. The growth of touring and growing market for guidebooks promised income in a way that the uncertain market for poetry did not. Wordsworth began with a financial motive, and abruptly lost interest in producing his own guide in late 1813 when Lord Holland arranged the stipend of £100 per annum as commissioner of stamps for Westmoreland, thus freeing the poet to pursue *The Recluse* project fulltime. This seems to be the practical reason for Wordsworth not returning to the fragment, although it was almost certainly set aside two years previously in 1811. That said, the philosophical grounding promised by the fragment remained unrealized in the 1820s, when Wordsworth produced the various iterations of *A Guide through the Lakes*. A letter to Jacob Fletcher from February 25, 1825 shows that he never stopped turning the problem over, nor did he overcome his sense of frustration:

> I will dismiss this, I fear tedious, subject [the inherent picturesqueness of objects] with one remark which will be illustrated at large, if I execute my intention — viz — that our business is not so much with objects as with the law under which they are contemplated. The confusion incident to these disquisitions [including his own unpublished disquisition] has arisen principally from not attending to this distinction. We hear people perpetually disputing whether

> this or that thing be beautiful or not — sublime or otherwise, without being aware that the same object may be both beautiful and sublime, but it cannot be felt to be such at the same moment — but I must stop —[13]

Wordsworth's efforts to make universal and permanent his experienced affection for the Langdale Pikes from a near-infinite range of potential prospects caused him to struggle toward an Idealist solution wherein we discover our cognitive grandeur and potential. He ultimately pulled away from this solution, however, due to the risk that such philosophical discourse might threaten the intense affection that commenced the process of enquiry in the first place. Wordsworth abandoned the ambition of producing a treatise for two reasons: he could not formulate an adequate account of "the sublime & the beautiful," and, more crucially, he feared that, in attempting to pick apart the reality of lived experience, experience itself could be compromised & lost.

Alan Vardy
Hunter College and the Graduate Center
CUNY

13. "To Jacob Fletcher, February 25, 1825," *The Letters of William and Dorothy Wordsworth*, Vol. III, 2nd Edition, eds Alan G. Hill & Ernest de Selincourt (1978) 322.

TEXTUAL NOTES & ALIA

NOTE ON THE TEXTS

Overall, the texts herein have been scrupulously replicated from the Oxford edition of Wordsworth's *Prose Works*; however, the following minor alterations have been made:

single quote marks for poem titles & quotes have been changed to double quote marks;

the line numbers given by the editors in the original Oxford edition have not been sustained for two reasons: first, they do not correspond to line numbers in the original manuscript; second, as noted above and outlined in detail in Vardy's introduction, new research has demonstrated that the order of the texts as conceived by Wordsworth is different from what was established by Owen & Smyser, who adopted the layout of Gordon Wordsworth, grandson of the poet. Ergo, all line numbers are intrinsic to our edition;

proper nouns have been capitalized where need be;

finally, the typographic conventions of the Oxford edition have not been followed but have been recast to correspond to our house style.

Wordsworth's ſpelling conventions have been suſtained.

Although several of the texts mentioned in the following manuscript key are not included in our edition (*Select Views*, et cetera), the key has been included in its entirety since many if not most of the manuscripts it mentions are referenced in the notes to the principal texts of our edition as well as in the commentaries.

The commentaries in the Appendix are by Owen and Smyser, as are the manuscript key, abbreviations, sigla, and the footnotes to both "Hawkshead & the Ferry" and "The Sublime & the Beautiful."

EDITING PROCEDURES

We preserve the manuscript spellings and abbreviations, with all their inconsistencies, where the manuscript lacks pointing, we silently insert it for the sake of intelligibility, but wherever we alter a mark of punctuation, we record that alteration in a textual note: although we have endeavored to preserve all deletions, we have not recorded the striking out and the immediate rewriting of identical words and phrases; we have also not recorded transpositions within a sentence of identical words, phrases, and clauses, and only rarely have we recorded the fact that some of the text was inserted, usually by means of a caret, at the very moment of composition. A table of sigla used in the textual notes will be found on XLX.

The numbering of the manuscripts in the Wordsworth Library at Grasmere, both those which we edit and those to which we briefly refer, is what will some day, no doubt, be called "Old Style." New numbers were assigned to all the manuscripts after this edition had gone into page proof, but scholars seeking to examine the manuscripts at Grasmere will find there a table of correspondences for the old and new numbering.

A note from Owen & Smyser, excerpted from the "Preface" to the first edition of Wordsworth's *Prose Works*.

The text for the *Guide* is that of the fifth edition, the last edition to be revised by Wordsworth: *A Guide through the District of the Lakes in the North of England* (1835). (For a bibliographical description, see Healey, item 93). The first edition, which appeared without the author's name, comprises three parts ("Introduction," "Section I," and "Section II") of Joseph Wilkinson's *Select Views* in Cumberland, Westmoreland, and Lancashire (1810). Because one part ("Section II") differs extensively from the corresponding passages in the four subsequent editions, we print it separately, with its own textual notes, under the title *Select Views*. But the other two parts of this first edition are preserved in the text and textual apparatus of the *Guide*. Textual notes also include variants from the second, third, & fourth editions, and from one manuscript in the Wordsworth Library. We here give, in chronological order, all the sources represented in the textual notes to the *Guide*:

1810 = "Introduction" and "Section I" in Joseph Wilkinson, *Select Views in Cumberland, Westmoreland, and Lancashire* (1810). See Healey, item 489; for a more detailed bibliographical description, see R.F. Metzdorf, *The Tinker Library* (1959) item 2337.

MS. = MS. Prose 30, written on white or ivory paper, with a watermark of 1810, is an early version of 858–979 ("As the comparatively ... internal springs"). The pages measure 7½ in. wide x 12 in. long; pages [1r]–[2r] are filled, but there are only nine lines of text on page [2v]. The hand in 858–79 ("As the ... native wood") is Mary Wordsworth's, but thereafter it is probably Dorothy Wordsworth's. Giving matter not in *Select Views*, the manuscript must have been written for the 1820 edition, for it is often significantly like 1820 and unlike the three later editions (e.g., see textual nn., 886, 888, 890, 897–8, 900–3, 905, 947–8, 952–9).

But it is also sometimes unique (e.g., see textual nn., 858, 863, 871, 878, 893, 950); either corrections were made in the proof sheets of 1820, or this manuscript was superseded by a revised copy now lost. (Once it is like 1822 and unlike 1820 (textual n., 865), and once it is like 1823 and unlike 1820 and 1822 (textual n., 951), but these two occurrences are no doubt accidental.)

1820 = *Topographical Description of the Country of the Lakes in the North of England*, in *The River Duddon ... and Other Poems* (1820) 213–323. See Healey, item 52.

1822 = *A Description of the Scenery of the Lakes in the North of England* (1822). See Healey, item 65.

1823 = *A Description of the Scenery of the Lakes in the North of England* (1823). See Healey, item 73.

Textual notes do not record our corrections of obvious misprints; nor do they record differences in spelling & punctuation, except where we alter the text of 1835 in favor of an earlier edition.

For the two parts of *Select Views* preserved in the text and textual notes of the *Guide*, no manuscript sources survive. But for that part ("Section II") which we print separately, manuscript variants do survive, and they are now published for the first time in our textual notes to *Select Views*. These manuscripts are almost inextricably related to other manuscripts, also in the Wordsworth Library, which constitute an unfinished work, hitherto unpublished. This unfinished work we now publish in two parts; for one part we choose the title "An Unpublished Tour," and for the other part we retain the title "The Sublime & the Beautiful," which the Library has given this manuscript. Before describing the individual manuscripts, we indicate by the following list the relationship between all the related manuscripts and Wordsworth's published & unpublished writings:

MSS. Prose 19: "An Unpublished Tour" (*U.T.*) 1–356.

MSS. Prose 20: *Select Views* (*S.V.*) 1–21, 46–58, 66–76; *U.T.* 357–557; two parts of a note to *The River Duddon* (*P.W.* iii.509–10, 515).

MSS. Prose 21: *U.T.* 558–812.

MSS. Prose 22: *U.T.* 812–1104.

MSS. Prose 23: *U.T.* 1105–591.

MSS. Prose 24: *S.V.* 89–200.

MS. Prose 25: *S.V.* textual n., 307/8.

MSS. Prose 26: *S.V.* 382–413; *U.T.* (MS. *A*) 1592–787.

MSS. Prose 27: *S.V.* 576–724.

MSS. Prose 28: "The Sublime & the Beautiful."

MS. Prose 29: *S.V.* 414–525.

MSS. Prose 30: Guide, 858–979 (described above).

MSS. Verse 57: *U.T.* 1592–787; *U.T.*, textual n., 1591/2.

With MSS. Prose 19–30 Gordon Wordsworth, grandson of the poet, has left a note describing the condition of these manuscripts when he first came upon them: "Tattered, torn, crumpled and subjected to frequent alterations and revisions, the sheets of flimsy paper were found rolled up in an untidy bundle with all their sequence lost." To Gordon Wordsworth the present editors are deeply indebted, for with patience and judicious care he sorted the manuscripts and arranged them in sequence. Except for ignoring deletions and early versions, he also transcribed in longhand MSS. Prose 19, 21, 22, 23, 25, 26, and those portions of MSS. Prose 20 and 24, which *Select Views* omitted entirely.

His transcript, preserved with the manuscripts, has been extremely valuable to us, for the originals are often very difficult to decipher. Because it would increase too much the bulk of our textual notes, we have not indicated the numerous words, and even phrases, which his transcripts have helped us to read, nor do we note the occasional passages where we have been able to correct his reading. But wherever we are uncertain of the text, we give in our apparatus his tentative reading (*G.W.*), if it differs from ours.

With a few exceptions, the manuscripts are in several respects strikingly alike; by a description of those elements which are common to MSS. Prose 19, parts of 20, 21–3, 25–9, we shall reduce the length and complexity of our subsequent descriptions of the individual manuscripts. Where a manuscript differs in any way from the general rule, as summarized here, we shall, of course, describe in detail that difference.

Although Wordsworth's hand appears frequently, most of the manuscripts are in the hand of Mary Wordsworth. When Mary was serving as the amanuensis, her hand sometimes shows signs of haste and becomes difficult to read, and especially so when the dictation called for immediate revision; but at other times her hand is clear, and then there are signs either: *(a)* that she is copying from an almost illegible first or second draft, which had been dictated to her or written out by Wordsworth himself; or *(b)* that she is taking dictation from a draft read to her by Wordsworth, who calls for occasional emendations in the course of dictating the draft. Wordsworth's hand, normally somewhat difficult, is here especially so; it is not unusual for one of these manuscripts to consist of several paragraphs dictated to Mary, then a few sentences in Wordsworth's hand, and then either new dictation, or an immediate copying by Mary of what Wordsworth had just written, followed by new dictation.

When the first draft, with its many false starts, its deletions and repetitions, and its reordering of identical phrases, is immediately rewritten in the same manuscript, we call the first draft MS. *A* and record its variants only when they contain matter that does not reappear in the rewritten copy. MS. *A* may vary in length from a whole separate page, as in MS. Prose 19[b], to a short paragraph or a few detached sentences.

But it should be emphasized here that, with the exception of MSS. Prose 20^{a}–20^{d} and Prose 24, no manuscript is a clean copy, and, with the same two exceptions, all manuscripts are incomplete or unfinished in one way or another.

The bulk of the manuscripts is written on the same kind of paper: a light-weight bluish-grey paper, impressed with horizontal chain lines 1 in. apart, a watermark of 1806, and a simple design that looks somewhat like an anchor. The full sheet measured 17¼ in. wide x 21 in. long. From two such sheets where the cutting was incomplete (MSS. Prose 19^{d} & 25), it is easy to see how the pages of various size were made: invariably the full sheet was folded horizontally at the middle & then slit or cut at the fold; after the cutting, the paper took half a dozen different forms:

1. A two-page unfolded half-sheet, 10½ in. wide x 17¼ in. long.
2. A four-page leaflet, 8⅝ in. wide x 10½ in. long, made from a half-sheet folded once.
3. A six-page leaflet, 8⅝ in. wide x 10½ in. long, made by inserting a quarter-sheet into a four-page leaflet.
4. An eight-page leaflet, 8⅝ in. wide x 10½ in. long, made from the full sheet, after being cut, as usual, at the center fold.
5. A sixteen-page leaflet, 8⅝ in. wide x 10½ in. long, made by folding together four half-sheets.
6. A quarter-sheet, made by cutting a half-sheet, or an irregular piece of paper torn or cut from either a full sheet or a half-sheet.

The measurements we have just given should be regarded as theoretical. If the paper had been cut exactly and folded evenly, the measurements would be correct, but actually slight variations in the cutting and folding, in addition to damages done to the edges by breaks and tears, have made almost all the pages slightly uneven: for example, the most commonly used four-page leaflet may have pages measuring 8½ in. wide at the top & 8 in. wide at the bottom, or 10 in. long on the left margin and 10¼ in. long on the right. In our descriptions of the individual manuscripts, the paper and the form and size of the sheet or leaflet are all as we have here described, unless otherwise specified.

In our descriptions of the individual manuscripts, the Arabic number (e.g., MSS. Prose 21) is the number assigned by the Wordsworth Library to a collection, or folder, of manuscripts. For convenience and clarity in referring to a particular manuscript within a collection, we attach to the Library number a superior lower case letter (e.g., MS. Prose 21^{b}).

As Mary Moorman (ii. 157) has pointed out, Wordsworth had told Lady Holland as early as August 1807 that he was "preparing a manual to guide travelers in their tour amongst the Lakes."[1] Mrs. Moorman thinks that this statement to Lady Holland strangely contradicts Wordsworth's firm rejection, in the following year, of Pering's request that he should write a description of the Lake District scenery, but the contradiction is surely more apparent than real. For Wordsworth "a manual to guide travelers" would not have been the same thing as "a formal delineation" of "this sublime and beautiful region," to quote again from his letter to Pering. After successfully completing such a delineation in his "Introduction" to Wilkinson's "expensive undertaking," it is understandable that he should revive the notion of preparing a "Guide" to fill out a separate — and possibly even more profitable — publication of his own.

Manuscripts in the Wordsworth Library show that he did, in fact, undertake such a composition. These manuscripts, which in our edition are entitled "An Unpublished Tour" and "The Sublime & the Beautiful," were all left unfinished; essentially, they are first, second, and occasionally third drafts for a work apparently soon abandoned. (For a description of the manuscripts, see Owen & Smyser, 137–49.) There is no date anywhere on the manuscripts, and we have found only one external reference to the work in progress, but we believe that the composition was not earlier than September 1811 and that it ceased about November 1812. The reason why we believe the manuscripts could not have been written before September 1811 is that, in writing about Donnerdale, Wordsworth incorporated into his new writing a part of an 1809 manuscript, transcribed for Wilkinson by Sara Hutchinson; in the course of expanding this section of the "old letter" — for that is

1. *The Journal of Elizabeth Lady Holland*, ed. The Earl of Ilchester (1908) ii. 231.

the way Wordsworth now refers to the manuscripts of *Select Views* — he adds details about the churchyard at Ulpha Kirk which he had acquired during a visit to it at the end of August or the beginning of September 1811. For example, in 1809, for *Select Views*, Wordsworth wrote of Ulpha Kirk: "A pleasing Epitaph, the only one in the place if I remember will be found affixed to the wall of the Church. This wild Count[ry was] once frequented by Druids ..."; at this point the "Unpublished Tour" manuscript was sewn directly over the "old letter," and the passage was then expanded to include not only a quotation of the eight-line epitaph but also the following new information: "This Tombstone, erected by a father to a Daughter who died at the age of one & twenty, is the only record in the Church yard, except that a Person has availed himself of the naked surface of a corner stone of the Chapel rudely to engrave thereon a brief notice of One who is buried near it. This wild country was once frequented by Druids ..." (L7.T. 472–7 and textual n. 461). Obviously, between 1809 and the writing of "An Unpublished Tour" Wordsworth had not only revisited the church but also jotted down the epitaph and observed other details. This he did at the end of August or the beginning of September 1811 on his way home from a month spent at the seaside with his wife and two youngest children (see *M.T.* i.499–503). In recounting to Sara Hutchinson the homeward journey, Wordsworth wrote: "Mary and I returned from Duddon Bridge, up the Duddon & through Seathwaite, the children with Fanny taking the direct road through Coniston. We dined in the Porch of Ulpha Kirk, and passed two Hours there and in the beautiful churchyard" (*M.T.* i.509). The two hours spent at Ulpha Kirk are clearly reflected in the expanded manuscript of "An Unpublished Tour."

How soon, or how long, it was after this visit to Ulpha Kirk that Wordsworth began writing his new guide we do not know, but by the following summer he must have written enough to tell Samuel Rogers something about it during the latter's visit to Windermere in August, when the two men were seeing each other often.[2] Sometime in the early

2. *See M.Y.* ii.42, 45.

winter Wordsworth wrote Rogers a letter which was all too promptly destroyed, as Rogers's reply on 9 January 1813 makes evident: "Upon my return from the North Pole yesterday, I found your Letter lying upon my table to welcome me; & happy, I can truly say, I shall be to execute any Commission you may favor me with. You say the Work is in prose — &, so far I read — but unfortunately being called off in the middle of the letter, short as it was, when I returned, I found that my Sister by some unlucky mistake had burnt it. If you have not entrusted it to another, pray send it to me that I may begin my negotiation. I hope it is that which relates to your own Lakes & mountains. As for myself I have been idling away my life in the Highlands."[3]

By the time this letter reached Grasmere, Wordsworth had already put aside his unfinished work.

3. Rogers's unpublished letter is in the Wordsworth Library.

ABBREVIATIONS

Addison, *Spectator* — Joseph Addison, *The Spectator*, ed. D.F. Bond (1965)

Ad. L.B. — Advertisement to *Lyrical Ballads* (1798)

Burke, *Enquiry* — Edmund Burke, *A Philosophical Enquiry into the Origin of our Ideas of the Sublime and Beautiful*, ed. J.T. Boulton (1958)

Burke, *Reflections* — Edmund Burke, *Reflections on the Revolution in France*, in *Works* (1886)

Cintra — *Concerning ... The Convention of Cintra*

Clarke — James Clarke, *A Survey of the Lakes of Cumberland, Westmorland, and Lancashire*, 2nd edition (1789)

C.N.B. — *The Notebooks of Samuel Taylor Coleridge*, ed. Kathleen Coburn (1957–)

Edd. — Editors

E.E. — *Essays Upon Epitaphs*

Exc. — *The Excursion*, in *P.W.* v.

E.Y. — *The Letters of William and Dorothy Wordsworth: The Early Years, 1787–1806*, ed. Ernest de Selincourt; 2nd edition, revised by Chester L. Shaver (1967)

Fragments — Early Prose Fragments

Gerard, *Genius* — Alexander Gerard, *Essay on Genius* (1774)

Gerard, *Taste* — Alexander Gerard, *Essay on Taste* (1759)

Gilpin — William Gilpin, *Observations Relative Chiefly to Picturesque Beauty ... Particularly the Mountains, and Lakes of Cumberland, and Westmoreland*, 2nd edition (1788)

Guide — *A Guide through the District of the Lakes in the North of England*

G.W. — Gordon Wordsworth's transcript of *Guide* manuscripts in the Wordsworth Library

Healey — George Harris Healey, *The Cornell Wordsworth Collection* (1957)

Hutchinson, *Excursion* — William Hutchinson, *An Excursion to the Lakes in Westmoreland and Cumberland...* (1776)

Hutchinson, *History* — William Hutchinson, *The History of the Country of Cumberland* (1794)

I.F. note — Notes dictated by Wordsworth to Isabella Fenwick in 1843 and printed in *P.W.*

Journals — *Journals of Dorothy Wordsworth*, ed. Ernest de Selincourt (1941)

L.Y. — *The Letters of William and Dorothy Wordsworth: The Later Years*, ed. Ernest de Selincourt (1939)

Moorman, i. — Mary Moorman, *William Wordsworth, a Biography: The Early Years, 1770–1803* (1957)

Moorman, ii. — Mary Moorman, *William Wordsworth, a Biography: The Later Years, 1803–1850* (1965)

M.P. — *Modern Philology*

M.W., *Letters* — *Letters of Mary Wordsworth*, ed. Mary E. Burton (1958)

M.Y. — *Letters of William and Dorothy Wordsworth: The Middle Years*, ed. Ernest de Selincourt; 2nd edition, revised by Mary Moorman & Alan G. Hill (1969–70)

O.E.D. — Oxford English Dictionary

Owen — *Wordsworth's Preface to 'Lyrical Ballads,'* ed. W.J.B. Owen (1957)

P. 1815 — Preface to the Edition of 1815

P.L.B. — Preface to *Lyrical Ballads*

Prel. — *The Prelude*, ed. Ernest de Selincourt; 2nd edition, revised by Helen Darbishire (1959). The text of 1805 is cited unless otherwise stated.

P.W. — *Poetical Works of William Wordsworth*, ed. Ernest de Selincourt & Helen Darbishire (1940–9, & revised issues, 1952–9).

Railway — *Kendal and Windermere Railway*

Reed — Mark L. Reed, *Wordsworth: The Chronology of the Early Years* (1967)

Reynolds — Sir Joshua Reynolds, *Works* (1798)

R.M. — Reply to "Mathetes"

S.C. — S.T. Coleridge, *Shakespearean Criticism*, ed. T.M. Raysor (1960)

Subl. and Beaut. — The Sublime & the Beautiful

S.V. — *Select Views*

U.T. — An Unpublished Tour

West, *Antiquities* — Thomas West, *The Antiquities of Furness* (1774)

West, *Antiquities* — Thomas West, *The Antiquities of Furness*, ed. William Close (1805)

Wordsworth as Critic — W.J.B. Owen, *Wordsworth as Critic* (1969)

TABLE OF SIGLA & ABBREVIATIONS

AS USED IN THE TEXTUAL NOTES

MS.	the first version in the manuscript
MS.[2]	the second version or first correction
MS.[3]	the third version or first correction
A[2]	the second version or first correction of MS. *A*
[?]	an illegible letter or letters, or word or words
[? there]	the word may be *there*
[? there *or* their]	the word is either *there* or *their*
[there]	an editorial interpolation
273/4	occurring between lines 273 and 274
corr.	corrected
del.	deleted
ins.	inserted
om.	omitted
subs.	substituted

A SAMPLE NOTE

there 1822: their MS.: here MS.[2], 1810–20.

The first occurrence of *there* is in the edition of 1822; the first version of the manuscript reads *their* (we avoid the use of *sic*); the second version of the manuscript and the editions of 1810 to 1820 read *here*.

FRAGMENTS

HAWKSHEAD & THE FERRY

WANT OF TIME, impatience to be forward, & other causes will hurry the great Body of Tourists past this first halting-place which I have recommended. But I hope the account of these excursions from the beaten track will not be found uninteresting in the perusal, even by such as do not visit the spots described. We now fall in with the ordinary road & proceed to Windermere by way of Hawkshead.

Before we leave the plain of the Vale of Conistone, we pass a house, the appearance of which shews that it has formerly been the Residence of a substantial yeoman or Estatesman. The Building is irregular & being somewhat neglected & decayed is the more picturesque on that account. Tall fir trees rise up around it with stems naked as masts, & the umbrella-like shade of their tops spreads a gloom & majesty over the humble fabric & the old fashioned garden. It is curious to observe here (& elsewhere) what pains has been taken to clip the yew trees into grotesque forms. One of these before us has been fashioned into a rude

---

2 will ... Tourists MS.[2]: will have hurried most Travellers MS. ¶ 3 recommended MS.[2]: recommended to them MS. ¶ 5 *After* perusal MS. *deletes*: while to such as proceed more leisurely MS. ¶ 8 Before we leave MS.[2]: Ascending the hill from Conistone Lake MS. Vale MS.[2]: Valley MS. a house MS.[4]: some MS.: an old substantial MS.[2]: a Farm MS.[3]. *Faintly inserted in pencil is*: a not noble. ¶ 14 humble MS.[2]: ancient MS. ¶ 15 *After* trees MS *deletes*: of this ¶ 16 grotesque MS.[2]: fantastic MS. ¶ 16 *After* fashioned MS. *deletes*: a [? rude] [?] seat.

likeness of a Man presenting a fowling-piece, as if to alarm the Traveller passing along the road. We should not be justified in concluding that the beautiful or stately growth of the forest in their natural shape had no attractions for the eyes of our ancestors who were so studious to disfigure, by the shears, those trees which, being planted by the side of their own doors, came the most frequently under their notice. This waywardness is in truth a step in the progress of refinement by a tie less gross than that of necessity: Man is thus connected with living Nature.

Yet in a Country so beautifully framed & prodigally adorned one cannot but be surprized at these instances of a busy propensity; & the perverseness with which the dwellings often turn their backs upon the finest Landscapes, even where there is not an excuse of catching a little sunshine, seems to shew that — though utter insensibility or absolute indifference to the general forms of Nature does not exist in any state of society, however rude — a relish for fine combinations of Landscape is assuredly an acquired taste. Of this cool contempt for the proffered bounty of Nature we have a striking instance as we ascend the hill. A little above the Cottage just passed, stands a gentleman's House, preferring a view across the road & a blank hill side, with a patch [of] northern sky, to a noble prospect of the Lake stretching southward & which, tho' hidden from the house, may be seen from an alcove in the pleasure ground behind, at a short distance from the door. There are, I know, many persons not insensible to the beauties of scenery who, in the choice of a scite for their residence, would rather avoid than seek a fine prospect from their windows, even if it could be procured

---

18 concluding MS.[2]: inferring MS. ¶ 19 *After* that MS. *deletes*: a tree ¶ 20 who were so MS.[3]: who took from MS.: who took so much pains MS.[2].* ¶ 26 instances MS.[2]: uncouth [*faintly del. with pencil*] instances MS. ¶ 29 shew] *Faintly altered in pencil to*: shews ¶ 31 a relish *Edd.*: that a relish MS. ¶ 34 the hill MS.[3]: the hill with the road from the Cottage just past MS.: along the hill side MS.[2]. ¶ 35 preferring MS.[2]: fronting the road MS. of *Edd.*: *om.* MS. ¶ 36 prospect MS.[2]: view MS. ¶ 37 & which, tho' MS.[3]: & which is planted out behind MS.: but which MS.[2]. ¶ 38 *After* ground MS. *deletes*: a few hundred [? yards] at *Edd.*: in at MS. door MS.[2]: house door MS. ¶ 39 scenery MS.[2]: Nature MS.

with a southern aspect & without the price of exposure to bleak winds. They think that it is more desirable to be tempted out of doors in search of entertainment of this kind, & apprehend that the best display of Nature's wealth would tire the mind, if constantly obtruded on the sight. But this weariness or indifference cannot ensue without a defect in the mind itself, for a landscape is a living thing, & the varieties of nature — infinite in themselves — are no where more affectingly exhibited than in the visionary regions of distance. How many splendid appearances of the sun rising or setting upon the sea or among distant mountain tops — how many phenomena of lights & shadows, of glorious vapours, & showers & storms coming in and clearing up are lost to those who have no chance of seeing these changes but when wandering out of doors! The most soothing house prospect is not an adequate recompence for the scanty allowance which from its seclusion it must necessarily yield of these grand exhibitions. In the choice of a situation, let sunshine & shelter be deemed indispensable, for tho' they may not be necessary to youth & to those who are in vigourous health, yet accidents of sickness & the unavoidable chillness of old age require this comfort & protection. But if where a comprehensive picture, visible from the window & brought even to the fire side, may be united with these primary recommendations, it is an error not to accept what the situation offers, tho' the reasons for the refusal may not actually imply what they will certainly have the appearance of — a sullenness against Nature. I have already contended that we are bound by the laws of taste not to disfigure a beautiful Country, or break in upon its composure by flaring edifices placed injuriously to the feelings of others for supposed advantages of our own; & I have already protested against that craving for extensive prospect which would

---

43 more desirable MS.[2]: better MS. ℂ 44 the best display MS.[2]: the most beautiful exhibitions MS. ℂ 45 *After* sight MS. *deletes*: but [this effect cannot *del.*] though I have already protested ... *and continues as in 67–73, where we will record the variants.* ensue without MS.[2]: follow w MS. ℂ 51 lights & shadows MS.[2]: storms & [? meteors] MS. ℂ 62 not to accept MS.[2]: to turn away from MS. ℂ 66 placed injuriously MS.[2]: improperly placed MS. ℂ 67 own; & *Edd.*: own. & MS.

prompt the builder to fix his habitation where it may stare & be stared at, after the manner of a trio of houses in a certain county which, from the absurdity of their appearance in this respect, have been severally nick-named by the Country-people Glare-at-'em, Glare-thro'-'em, & Glare-o'er-'em. With those, therefore, to whom I am recommending extent of prospect, this opinion will have a better chance of being listened to, and the giver of it may claim credit for sharing their aversion to this kind of exposure & for sympathy with the modesty of their feelings.

A ¼ of a mile higher up the hill, near some Cottages called Hollinbank, will be found, both above & below the road, excellent points from which to take a last view of the Lake & Vale of Conistone we have left.

A mile farther on, we begin to descend into the Vale of Hawkshead, having from the high ground a sight of the upper part of Windermere stretching to the left. In the first cluster of houses we come to, named Hawkshead hill, stands a meeting-house by the road side, belonging to a congregation of Anabaptists, called by the Country people who are not of their own persuasion "Whigs." The Building is mean, & on the outside has so little to distinguish it as a place of worship that one might think it had been so constructed in an intolerant age for the purpose of avoiding notice; but this Conventicle is endowed with Lands that produce a respectable income for the Minister. I [? point] the Passenger's attention to that object because this is the only establishment of the kind that I know of among these Mountains. Behind runs a streamlet which

69 where MS.^{2}: upon a hill top or high on a naked hill side where MS. ¶ after MS.^{2}: in MS. ¶ 70 certain MS.^{2}: neighbouring MS. ¶ 73 o'er-'em. MS.^{2}: o'er-en; yet MS.* ¶ 74 prospect MS.^{2}: prospect from their windows as many MS. ¶ 75 sharing MS.^{2}: being in sympathy MS. ¶ 77 near some Cottages called MS.^{2}: at a place called MS.** ¶ 82 come to MS.^{2}: come to on the left MS. ¶ 83 *After* road side MS. *deletes*: which having little of the appearance ¶ 85 *After* "Whigs" MS. *deletes*: behind this ¶ 87 think MS.^{2}: think that MS. so constructed MS.^{2}: erected MS. ¶ 88–89 but this ... produce MS.^{2}: Lands are settled upon the Minister doing duty here from which proceeds MS. ¶ 89 point MS.^{2}: mention this MS. ¶ 91 among *Edd.*: in MS.: [among *del.*] MS.^{2} ¶ 91 runs a *Edd.*: [? there *or* this] is a [small Cemetery reservoir *del.*] runs streamlet MS.

is occasionally diverted into a reservoir wherein Adults are dipped, some coming from a considerable distance for this purpose. A little detached from the building lies also a small Cemetery, with one low headstone in the centre. The inscription is scarcely to be traced on account of the lichens that have crept over the stone. This obscure burial place is of a character peculiarly melancholy. The ground is humbly fenced, like [? any] of the neighbouring fields, & not a tree planted to dignify or adorn it. But among this little company of graves, how much mortal weariness is laid at rest, how many anxieties are stilled, what tender scruples & fearful apprehensions removed forever!

To this congregation, who [?] [? devout worship], belonged many years ago a Man oppressed by religious melancholy, whose residence was at the head of the wild valley of Langdale. One day he rose up from the table where he had been reading his Bible & dropped some words intimating that he should be seen no more. It is remarkable that those who heard him speak to this effect were not induced from apprehension of some ill consequence to follow his steps. But as he did not return, search was made after him when too late, & continued both in his own neighbourhood & thro distant parts of the Country; no tidings could be gained of him. It happened, however, that long after while a Shepherd was passing along the bank of a rugged gill near the head of Langdale, his dog brought from below a bone which the Shepherd might not perhaps have noticed, but a Person who was with him suggested that it belonged, as he phrased it, to the body of a Christian. Upon this, they descended into the ghyll, & other human bones were found

93 *After* purpose MS. *deletes*: not [?]ing which occasions, does not meet with much [? respect] from the minds [?] detached MS.^{2}: detached only MS. ¶ 95–6 is scarcely … stone MS.^{2}: is difficult to read almost overgrown with lichens — this is a solitary & melancholy spot MS. ¶ 96 burial place MS.^{2}: burial place with the small company of graves which it contains has a MS. ¶ 98 any MS.^{2}: one MS. ¶ 98 not a tree]* ¶ 98 dignify *Edd.*: dignity MS. ¶ 100 is MS.^{2}: here is MS. ¶ 109 him MS.^{2}: the Man MS. ¶ 109–10 & continued … & thro MS.^{2}: not only in his own neighbourhood but in MS. ¶ 112 along MS.^{2}: by MS. ¶ 116 they … ghyll MS.^{2}: search was made MS.

that had been cast up by the torrent among the rocks & bushes. These were carefully collected up, & it not being doubted that they were the remains of this unhappy Man who had disappeared, they were brought to be interred in this burial ground. As the circumstances had made much impression in the neighbourhood, a large company attended, and a sermon was delivered from the text "How can these dry bones be quickened." Doubtless, the Preacher, in treating the subject of the resurrection of the Body, would not overlook upon this occasion that most sublime passage of Ezekiel where the Prophet speaks of himself as set down in the valley of dry Bones. "And he said unto me, Son of Man, can these bones live? And I answered, O Lord God, Thou knowest."

Proceeding, we are soon after greeted by the white Church of Hawkshead standing conspicuously on a Hill, a chearful salutation & particularly so for those whose minds it may relieve from such serious reflections as the [*blank*] House of worship which we have left & its appurtenances will naturally lead to.

At the foot of the hill within ½ a mile of Hawkshead stands by the road side an ancient Building, named Hawkshead Hall, which yet retains in the stone work of the windows & gateways some interesting fragments of gothic architecture. In this house the Abbot of Furness kept residence by one or more Monks, who performed divine service in the Church & other parochial duties in that neighbourhood. There still remains a court room over the gate-way where the bailiff of Hawkshead held court & distributed justice in the name of the Abbot.

Passing over Gallow-barrow, a low hill probably so named from its having formerly been a place where criminals were executed under the jurisdiction of the Abbot, we arrive at the little Market Town of

117 among] *altered from* amongst ℭ 118 collected MS.[2]: gathered MS. ℭ 122 delivered from the text MS.[2]: delivered upon the occasion from the text MS.: preached by the Minister upon the occasion from the words as I have been told MS. *A.* ℭ 124 would not overlook MS.[2]: would remind his [? listeners *del.*] [? hearers] MS.* ℭ 134 Building, named MS.[2]: Building on the left called MS. ℭ 135 stone work of MS.[2]: window MS.** ℭ 141 Gallow-barrow MS.[2]: Gallow-barrow hill & [?] MS. named MS.[2]: named during MS. ℭ 143 little MS.[2]: small MS.***

Hawkshead, pleasantly situated at the foot of a range of small cultivated or woody hills rising irregularly behind each other & backed by a ridge of bare fells. On the top of the hill which screens the Town stands the Church, overlooking the Valley, the southern extremity of which is filled by a Lake called Esthwaite water. Immediately under the Church yard on the eastern side stands the Grammar School house, founded & liberally endowed by Archbishop Sandes, a Native of this neighbourhood.

The munificence of this Prelate & the partiality which would naturally be felt by those amongst whom he had been born for one who rose to so high a station in the Church would perhaps have some tendency to reconcile the rude people of this district to the changes made by the reformation, from which at first they had been extremely averse, not only for reasons generally felt through the nation, [but also] on account of their attachment to their ancient Lords, the Abbots of Furness. A fisherman in this town, who stiled himself the Earl of Poverty, was one of the most conspicuous leaders in the famous pilgrimage of Grace which disturbed the northern Counties in the time of Henry the Eight. How far this neighbourhood was committed in that insurrection & with what regret the people then looked back upon the institutions that had been destroyed may be inferred from a perusal of the following Summons from the chief Captains of the Commonalty assembled in pilgrimage:

> To the Commyns of Hawkside Parish, Bailiffs, or Constables, with all the Hamletts of the same.
>
> Welbeloved we greet you well; whereas our brother Poverty, (the fisherman above spoken of) & our brother Rogers goith forward, is openly for the aide & assistance of your faith & holy church & for the reformation of such abbeys & monasteries, now dissolved

---

145 irregularly MS.[2]: irregularly in [? stages] MS. ❡ 147 Valley MS.[2]: Valley towards MS. ❡ 151 *After* Prelate MS. *deletes*: the high station he rose to in the Church the dignity ❡ 152 had been MS.[2]: were MS. ❡ 156 but also *Edd.*: *om.* MS. ❡ 160 in the time of MS.[2]: in Henry the eighth MS. ❡ 161–2 with what regret MS.[2]: what interest the People took in MS. ❡ 163 from MS.[2]: by MS. ❡ 163 *After* Summons MS. *deletes*: No.

> & suppressed without any just cause. Wherefore gudde brethers, forasmuch as our sayd brederyn hath send to us for ayde & help, wee do not only effectually desire you, but also under the paine of deadly sinne we commaunde you, evry of you, to be at the stoke greene beside Hawkeside kirke, the Saturday next, being the XXVIII day of October, by XI of the clock, in your best array; as you will make answer before the heigh judge at the dreadful day of dome, & in the payne of pulling downe your houses, & leasing of your gudd[?s], & your bodies to be at the Capteyns will: for at the place afforesaid, then & there, yee & we shall take further directions concerning our faith, so far decayed, & for gudde & laudable customes of the country, & such naughty inventions & strange articles now accepted & admitted, so that our said brothers bee subdued, they are lyke to goe furthwards to utter undoing of the comynwealth.

What particular spot of ground the illiterate Sansculottes & Luddites of that day were invited & commanded to meet upon, in order to reinforce their Brother Poverty, I am unable to point out, but, thanks to the good Archbishop, Stoke green is probably now lost in the Schoolmaster's Orchard or in some enclosure that has since daily resounded with more agreeable tumults than prevailed in that discontented assembly — the noise of a numerous band of happy Schoolboys engaged in their sports & gamesome contests.

Along the eastern end of the Church runs a stone seat, a place of resort for the old people of the Town, for the sickly, & those who have leisure to look about them. Here sitting in the shade or in the sun, they

---

187 *After* ground MS. *deletes*: [under the *del.*] in the neighbourhood of the Church was fixed upon for the place of meeting where ¶ 189 point out MS.[2]: say MS. ¶ 191–2 more agreeable MS.[2]: other MS. than *Edd.*: then MS. ¶ 193 engaged in MS.[2]: occupied with MS. ¶ 194 *After* contests MS. *deletes*: [? along] [? From] Caprice & fashion are suffered to [? interfere] in the most serious concerns of body & mind [a physician shall lose *del.*] the practice of a physician shall fall away without any abatement of industry on his part or proof [given *del.*] afforded of want of skill. ¶ 197 *After* them MS. *deletes*: to.

talk over their concerns, & a few years back were amused by the gambols & exercises of more than a 100 Schoolboys, some playing soberly on the hill top near them, while others were intent upon more boisterous diversions in the fields beneath. This public seat has indeed many recommendations, & if those who frequent it cast their eyes upon the lofty Mountains which rise above the immediate boundary of this Vale towards the North, they will there often behold movements & changes of a more slow & tranquil character, which, however, it requires some degree of imagination to take an interest in. Upon a Summer afternoon cast with shadows of the clouds, deep & determined, the fells of Kirkstone & Rydale head appear from this seat like a tract of chosen ground upon which detachments of a silent army are maneuvering; positions are taken up and relinquished; the Spectacle is entertaining & the law by which the changes are governed is a mystery. If I have lingered too long upon this favorite old resting place, the Reader will excuse a partiality produced by the recollections of more than 10 years of Boyhood & Youth passed in this Valley, a period during which neither the eye was inattentive nor the imagination torpid.

Within the Church is a stone Monument erected to the Parents of Archbishop Sandys, who are represented as recumbent figures side by side, a Latin inscription running like a band round the square Tablet upon which they are laid. Nor can I omit noticing that the Church

---

199 *After* Schoolboys MS. *deletes*: spread over the ground [below them *del.*] beneath their eyes ℂ 199 soberly MS.[2]: soberly at their side MS. while MS.[2]: & MS. ℂ 201 diversions MS.[2]: amusements MS. *After* beneath MS. *deletes*: [? Improvements] & changes little [? obscure] of a more tranquil character [carried out by *del.*] & which perhaps it requires some degree of imagination to take an interest in are ℂ 201–211 This public ... mystery] *Possibly deleted.* ℂ 204 behold MS.[2]: be entertained by MS. ℂ 205 more slow MS.[2]: very different MS.* ℂ 208–209 seat like a tract of chosen ground ... are maneuvering; positions *Edd.* (*cf. preceding note*). MS. *seems to read*: seat [?] upon which detachments of a silent army maneuvering upon a tract of chosen ground — positions ℂ 210 relinquished MS.[2]: relinquished by a law which MS. ℂ 212 old resting place MS.[2]: ground MS. ℂ 212 a MS.[2]: my MS. ℂ 215 *After* torpid MS. *deletes*: Before we quit Hawkshead it may be worth while to add that ℂ 216 Within MS.[2]: In MS. is MS.[2]: [?] seen MS. ℂ 219–220 the Church contains MS.: there is MS. *A.***

contains a plain marble slab sacred to the memory of Eliz. Smith, buried here a few years ago.

Of this extraordinary young Person memoirs have been published, & from them & from [her] own letters & compositions it appears that her acquisitions in learning & science were such as would have done honour to professed Scholars, & what is more remarkable were made in secret by unassisted efforts, triumphing over difficulties which to a less ardent zeal would have been insuperable. Till after her death the measure of these attainments was unknown to those with whom she daily conversed & even to her most intimate friends, so that she appears to have walked thro' the world by the side of her companions like a being of superior Nature — in no unworthy disguise but still that of human shape — who is not discovered till the wings that declare him to be of celestial origin are unfolded at his departure, & he is gone & hath left sadness & unavailing regret behind. This lamented young woman dwelt in the earlier part of her youth on the banks of the Wye, & the regret which by a mind tenderly alive to the beautiful in every thing must have been felt upon being compelled to relinquish the treasures of that favourite spot was, in course of time, alleviated by new attachments to scenes of nature still more beautiful & sublime, which her residence in this Country gave her an opportunity of forming. The loftiest peaks that were accessible to female feet had been trodden by her light steps, & the deepest dells were not unknown to her, & every nook of the scenes in the neighbourhood of Conistone thro' which I have led my Companion was especially to [*sic*] her affections. To the strength of these attachments she gave in her last illness a most moving testimony. For the restoration of her health, a milder climate had been recommended, & it happened one day while in a state of alarming debility she was inhaling

---

223 her *Edd.*: *om.* MS. compositions MS.[2]: fragments MS. ¶ 226 *After* efforts MS. *deletes*: supported with great [?] triumphing MS.[2]: triumphed MS. ¶ 228 measure MS.[2]: extent MS. was MS.[2]: were MS. to those MS.[2]: to her acquaintances MS. ¶ 229 appears MS.[2]: appears in this respect MS. ¶ 230 a being MS.[2]: a celestial MS. ¶ 232 shape MS.[2]: being MS. ¶ 233 gone MS.[3]: taken MS.: departed MS.[2]. ¶ 242 *After* scenes MS. *deletes*: we have.

the fresh air, within a tent placed at a small distance from her father's house upon a knoll on the sloping bank of Conistone Water, she was pressed to submit to this trial. To which entreaty, fixing her glistening eyes upon the landscape, one of the loveliest that the Vale affords, with an earnestness & even an impatience of voice & manner almost unnatural in her character, the sufferer answered that if she could not be well with such a heavenly sight before her, she could be well no where.

I have already noticed that the northern boundary of Hawkshead is overlooked by the Heights of Ambleside & Rydale; & leaving the Church yard & Town, as we cross the Vale on our way toward the Ferry house of Windermere, we see that its western barrier is overtopped by the mountain called the Old Man, whose rugged bosom, with the waterfalls which it embraces, enlivens & sets off by contrasts the smooth lake & fertile fields of Conistone, & whose summit crowns that picture which, if it did not supply earthly hope to this dying Maiden, at least soothed her pain, lifted up her spirits, & through the medium of perishable things reminded her, as by a faint reflexion, of regions maintained by the love of the Almighty in secure & undecaying beauty.

This Vale of Hawkshead is one of that class which within their own limits contain nothing but what is of humble character, yet possess considerable dignity borrowed from communication with Mountains that belong to other Vales. Looking back when we have reached the Lake

---

249 *After* Water MS. *deletes*: & is in view of one of the most lovely [landscapes *del.*] scenes which the Vale affords. ¶ 253 the sufferer MS.[2]: she MS. ¶ 255 Hawkshead MS.[2]: this Vale MS. ¶ 256 the Heights MS.[2]: the Mountains [of *del.*] above Ambleside & Rydale & as taking MS. ¶ 257 toward MS.[2]: to MS. ¶ 259 the mountain MS.[2]: the Fells of Coniston & in particular by the Old Man the Mountain which embosoms the waterfalls & rocks that MS. ¶ 260 *After* waterfalls MS. *deletes*: [? running] ¶ 261 & whose summit MS.[2]: & that summit of which MS. ¶ 262 *After* which MS. *deletes*: soothed the heart of this *After* hope MS. *deletes*: at least soothed this troubled spirit ¶ 263 pain MS.[2]: pain & MS. through MS.[2]: by MS. ¶ 265–66 *G.W. inserts the matter given at the beginning of our textual n. 140–150. Nothing that we can see in the text or on the manuscript justifies an insertion here.* ¶ 266 that class which within MS.[2]: those which in MS. ¶ 267 nothing ... character MS.[2]: few objects but those [?] which are of humble character but which have MS. ¶ 269 when we have reached MS.[2]: we see that as we approach MS.

of Esthwaite, we see that Langdale Pikes have reared themselves into notice. One of them from this point takes the form of a sugar loaf &, not less for its singularity than its majesty, makes an interesting background to a beautiful landscape, of which the white church of Hawkshead is a gay feature.

But hurrying forward to this scene, I have passed without notice a pool at the head of the Lake where if the wind had been up & had suddenly veered, we might have been startled by the sight of a curiosity — a floating grove in full sail. This moving Island does not appear & disappear, like the buoyant wonder of Derwent water, but navigates at all seasons the surface of this small pool, the trees that grow upon it serving it as masts & sails. There is no mystery in the origin of this unusual appearance, as it is plain that the platform with the trees upon it has been detached from the spungy ground that borders the pool & the winds will not suffer it to be reunited to the shore. I have not learned whether it increases in compass or diminishes.

Adjoining to this Pool, which is named Priest-pot, perhaps from some Ecclesiastic having been drowned in it, formerly stood a gibbet, upon which the body of some atrocious Criminal had been hung in Chains near the spot where his crime had been committed. Part of the Irons & some of the wood work remained in my memory. Think of a human figure tossing about in the air in one of these sweet Valleys.

---

270 reared MS.^{2}: lifted MS. ¶ 271 One of MS.^{2}: The form MS. ¶ 275 But ... scene MS.: But I have neglected to mention in its place a pool MS. *A*: But in my hastening forward to this scene MS. A^2. ¶ 276–78 Lake where ... floating MS., MS. A^2: Lake surrounded with spungy ground a piece of Water in no wise remarkable but that it contains a floating MS. *A*. ¶ 278–79 grove in ... but MS., MS. A^2: [island *del.*] Grove not one that appears like the famous one of Derwent Water MS. *A*. ¶ 279 navigates MS., MS. A^2: sails about MS. A. ¶ 280 at all seasons MS.^{2}: at all times MS.: *not in* MS. *A*. *After* pool MS. *A deletes*: as the wind shifts ¶ 282 unusual appearance MS., MS. A^4: moving Curiosity MS. *A*: appearance MS. A^2: phenom MS. A^3. ¶ 287 in it MS.^{2}: there MS. gibbet MS.^{2}: gibbet of which some of the wood work MS. ¶ 288 atrocious *Edd.*: attrocious MS. had been MS.^{2}: had [? for] been MS. ¶ 290 Think MS.^{2}: I should MS. ¶ 291 in the air MS.^{2}: [with the *del.*] upon the wind MS.

'Tis an object sufficiently fearful & repulsive upon Hounslow heath or in the solitudes of Salisbury Plain, but in a populous enclosure like this where no one could look round without being crossed by the sight — what a dismal annoyance! It seems as if no sense of humanity, no feeling for rural beauty could have existed in the minds of those who among their woods & fields could tolerate such a spectacle. At that time the marshy ground at the head of this lake used to resound with the doleful cry of the Bittern, which, by the bye, has never been heard in its ancient haunts since the great frost in 1740. This sound, blending with the whistling of the Hawk repairing hither from distant crags & the croaking of the carrion Crow & the Raven attracted by the suspended corpse, must have made a dismal chorus for the ears of Passengers, while the circumstances of the murder were yet fresh in memory, approaching along the several lanes which meet near the point where the gibbet stood. The heads of traitors, should the times unfortunately breed such offenders, would no longer be stuck up upon Temple Bar, nor their Quarters dispersed to strike terror from the gates of provincial Cities, & it would be well if this odious custom of exposing the Bodies of Criminals, of whatever description, were abandoned & all traces of this relic of barbarism had disappeared from the land. If such an exhibition, thro' long familiarity with it, can be looked at with indifference by the innocent & good, there is surely nothing gained, but such an effect is rather to be deplored. Whom can the ignominy of this exposure deter from wickedness? Surely not those from whose hand the most inhuman cruelties

---

292 'Tis an object MS.[2]: [how melancholy *del.*] tis a sight MS. or] *wrongly deleted.* ¶ 293 Plain, but MS.[2]: Plain or upon Hounslow heath MS. a MS.[2]: an MS. this MS.[2]: [? this *or* that] valley MS. ¶ 294 no one could MS.[2]: it must have been impossible to look round MS. being crossed MS.[2]: seeing it MS. ¶ 302–3 suspended corpse MS.[2]: dead body MS. ¶ 305 *After* stood MS. *deletes*: It would be well if all traces of this odious ¶ 307 stuck up MS.[2]: exposed MS. ¶ 308 from MS.[2]: upon MS. ¶ 310 this relic MS.[2]: it MS. *After* land MS. *deletes*: This practice is a [? reproach] to humanity & a reproach to civilization ¶ 313 there is MS.[2]: then it is MS. ¶ 314 deplored MS.[2]: regretted MS. ¶ 315 most inhuman cruelties MS.[2]: worst crime MS.

are to be apprehended! There is no place which a hardened villain would prefer for the perpetration of a murder to the foot of a gibbet, if it lay within his choice. He would select that very place in pride & bravado; & by such unaccountable impulses sometimes is man driven to action, & his unhappy mind is so subject to be visited by perverse thoughts that evil in the worst degree is often committed which would never have been dreamt of but for the injudicious means used to prevent it.

No vestiges probably now remain of the object which led me to these reflections, but I should be sorry to think that the pool is no longer frequented by a pair of beautiful Swans, long lived creatures which haunted it for many years & which sailing about on a windy day by the side of the floating Island would have made a romantic picture for the entertainment of any eye. This faithful pair & another pair equally faithful to each other divided the domain of Esthwaite Water & the pools & streams at the head & foot of it equally between them. An instance was never known of either couple encroaching upon the rights of the other. These beautiful Birds were a striking ornament to this small lake. The tranquil habits of swans and their gentle [? moods] suit the stillness of diffused water, so that these animals seemed placed more appropriately to their Natures and more happily upon lakes, where the element is kept within bounds, than upon Rivers subject to impetuous floods. Tame Swans were brought to Windermere, & the breed of them encouraged there several years ago. Upon [that] plain of water, so large in a general view, these inhabitants of the surface were

---

317 would prefer MS.[2]: would with so much pride & bravado select MS. ℭ 317–18 if it ... choice MS.[3]: where the MS.: if he had a MS.[2]. ℭ 318 that very place MS.[2]: the place MS. unaccountable MS.[2]: strange MS. ℭ 319 *After* action, & MS. *deletes*: so it often is ℭ 320 perverse thoughts MS.[2]: thoughts the opposite of those which MS. ℭ 323 No vestiges MS.[2]: [No *del.*] [all *del.*] No vestiges of th MS. ℭ 325 long MS.[2]: [? most] MS. ℭ 328 pair & MS.[2]: pair if still in existence MS. ℭ 331 couple encroaching MS.[2]: pair trespassing MS. ℭ 333 The *Edd.*: & the MS.: Their MS.[2]. *After* swans MS. *deletes*: suits the placid [?] gentle moods] *possibly* gentleness ℭ 338 Upon that plain *Edd.*: That plain MS.: Upon plain MS.[2]. ℭ 339 *After* water MS. *deletes*: is too large ℭ 339 these ... were MS.[2]: [? they became] MS.

insignificant, [but] meandering along the creeks & bays, there they appeared objects of importance. Upon Windermere they became numerous; their trespasses upon the fields bordering the lake being complained of, the breed was destroyed. Those of Esthwaite, fortunately for themselves & their admirers, did not multiply; being so few in numbers, their depredations were allowed, & in the hard season of winter several Persons took delight in occasionally carrying them food. I am writing of the Vale of Hawkshead from memory, & I will suppose that my old acquaintances, the faithful swans, are still in existence or that others have taken their place, enlivening the fore ground of the picture by the Lakeside to which we shall return. Their towering wings and snow white plumage harmonize with the white Church of Hawkshead, standing at some distance upon the hill and leading the eye to the hoary pikes of Langdale by which the horizon is bounded.

At the point where we have turned back upon this view, lies a slip of poor cultivated land, not much wider than the road itself. By this appropriation, which has not long been made, agriculture has gained little, and liberty & taste have lost much, for it has shortened a pleasant line of communication [?] [?] which the road on this side [? makes] with the lake. In the wall that bounds this obnoxious enclosure is yet to be seen the remnant of a decaying Yew tree within which some contemplative Man erected a seat. Here a wayworn traveller might have found a grateful resting-place, protected from the wind or the sun, for the boughs

---

340 *After* insignificant MS. *deletes*: but they were often seen to great advantage sailing about in little fleets but *Edd.*: and MS. *Cf. preceding note.* ¶ 341 they [*second*] MS.[2]: the breed MS. ¶ 341–2 *After* numerous MS. *deletes*: & the breed was destroyed in consequence of complaints made by the property owners of fields bordering the lake that property was injured [?] ¶ 342–3 being complained of, MS.[2]: were complained of & MS. ¶ 343 fortunately] *wrongly deleted.* ¶ 344 multiply MS.[2]: breed in this number from there MS. ¶ 349 enlivening MS.[2]: beautifying MS. ¶ 351 harmonize MS.[2]: harmonizing MS. ¶ 353 horizon MS.[2]: Landscape MS. ¶ 354 At the point where MS.: In front of the MS.[2] (*inserted and not deleted, but left incomplete in sense*). ¶ 355 poor MS.[2]: enclosed MS. *After* itself MS. *deletes*: divides the road from the water not wider than the water [*sic*] itself.* ¶ 357 *After* lost much MS. *deletes*: for it has destroyed a pleasant communication of the high road with.

had been trained to bend round the seat & almost embrace the Person who might occupy the seat within, allowing only an opening for the beautiful landscape. The narrow space between the yew tree & the Lake was scattered over with juniper, furze, heath, & wild time, a pretty range of nature's free ground ill exchanged for a worthless, misshapen field whose smooth surface renders more conspicuous the meagreness of the soil. These notices are minute, but to the loss [? in] the mind of such a Man as probably constructed the arbour that I have described might be [? Considerable] among Life's little changes, & prove a cause of daily regret.

Advancing, we come to the point where the Road for a short space still lies open to the Lake shore. The traveller may pause &, if on foot, he will be inclined to stretch himself on the slopes back of the common, where he may look round him at liberty, in a situation which, though it be low, will distinctly shew him the character of this Vale. We have already classed it among those of minor interest which make up for the deficiencies within [their] own circuit by borrowing grandeur & boldness from a distance, and we have slightly sketched the principal features in the view towards the North. [? From] The eastern side of the lake is [?] a [? tame] ridge almost covered with coppice woods, but as we are travelling immediately along its base, [? we see] too little of this form-

366 *After* time MS. *deletes*: [? This *or* these] primeval [? growth] converted into misshapened fields whose comparatively smooth surface renders more crude the meagreness of the soil ℂ 369 *After* loss MS. *deletes*: which these changes in] *possibly* to ℂ 370 might be MS.[2]: & who could MS. changes MS.[2]: [? things] MS. ℂ 372 Advancing MS.[2]: As MS. ℂ 373 *After* shore MS. *deletes*: we may look round us and repose at liberty here ℂ 375 look MS.[2]: repose MS. *After* liberty MS. *deletes*: We have already [slightly sketched *del.*] classed this Valley and [? their] the principal features as The view towards the north those which wanting bold & [? dignified] features within their [proper *del.*] own circuit must supply the deficiencies ℂ 377 those MS.[2]: those vales MS. ℂ 378 their own *Edd.*: own MS. ℂ 378 grandeur] *G.W. reads*: greatness ℂ 381 tame] *G.W. reads*: bare (cf. 1576.) almost MS.[2]: chiefly MS. ℂ 381 but as we are MS.[2]: as we have been MS. ℂ immediately MS.[2]: now MS. its base MS.[2]: the base of it MS. ℂ 382 we see *Edd.* (*G.W. reads* we see, *probably because the context calls for something like that, but we do not find these words in the manuscript. There seems to be one short illegible word.*) formless ridge] *G.W. reads*: formality.

less ridge to complain of it. The Western side is formed as if in contrast to this, being entirely broken from top to bottom into smooth [? round]-topped hills, which have a remarkable softness of appearance. These hills, with the hedge rows intersecting them in various directions, and several patches of wood in different positions upon all of them, impress, as has been observed, upon that side of the vale a peculiar character, and form some of the most delightful sheltered situations for houses that can well be imagined. There are no islands in Esthwaite water. But it has the further particularity of 2 large round peninsulas on opposite sides of the Lake, one of which by the form & the manner in which it is attached to the shore seems to have reminded some one's fancy of the human ear, for it is called Strickland-ears — perhaps instead of Strickland's ear the *s* being transferred to the end of the designation that the word may pass more easily off the tongue.

The ancient inhabitants have been attracted by the fitness & beauty of those scites for houses with which the Stranger whose words we have quoted was smitten, & he might have added to his description that the ground which he praises is scattered over with chearful & modest dwellings, standing removed from each other at distances that allow a domain of land to each sufficient for the maintenance of the family, yet of that small compass which indicates the moderate desires of the owner & affords the advantages, without the annoyance, of neighbourhood. But the *perfection* in which this characteristic beauty was here exhibited no longer exists; the old habitations of the country are beginning to be supplanted by fabrics which from their size require — what is not always to be obtained — an enlargement of boundary which did not

386 the] *possibly* their ¶ 388 as has been MS.^{2}: as some one MS. ¶ 390–1 in Esthwaite MS.^{2}: upon this Lake MS. But it MS.^{2}: but two MS.* ¶ 397 attracted by MS.^{2}: struck with MS. ** ¶ 400 chearful MS.^{2}: happy looking MS.*** ¶ 402 family MS.: household MS. *A*. yet MS.^{2}: but MS. which indicates the moderate MS.^{2}: that seems to express the moderate MS.: that seemed to express [? respect for *del.*] the moderate MS. *A*. ¶ 404 & MS.^{2}: & assuredly MS., MS. *A*. ¶ 404–5 *After* neighbourhood MS. *A deletes*: Such at least was the happy equality of [?] that nature & society had produced.**** ¶ 408 obtained MS.^{2}: obtained with MS.

press too closely upon their unambitious predecessors; & under these circumstances, that stile of building & arrangement of ground have been introduced that bespeak a transition from one state of society to another awkwardly & uneasily performed. Here within a circuit where the space of land capable of cultivation is so confined, one may be permitted to repine at such change, both for the suitableness, harmony, & happy equality that have been displaced, & for the disproportions & deformities which mark its commencement & will attend its progress.

They who peruse these pages at a distance from the scene may think that we have already lingered too long in a Vale of so little celebrity. By what has been said, I have wished to mark the character of Esthwaite lake as an individual spot, but the chief interest pertaining to it and to other lakes of the same class is of a general nature. Its waters are pure & crystalline; the breezes have room to play upon its surface, & the strong winds to agitate its depths. No finer network is woven than that which light airs frame of its liquid materials, & when its restlessness causes it to sparkle in the sunshine with diamonds, their myriads are not less brilliant than those which deck the stately breast of Windermere or Loch Lomond.

I need not speak of the Water fowl that resort to it from remote regions in winter, nor of the Swallows that wheel round it in summer & are reflected in its smooth mirror, nor of the Boats that glide along its [? even] bosom, nor of the sports of angling, bathing, or skating, which in the several seasons enliven it from centre to circumference.

---

410 that MS.[2]: the MS. ¶ 413 land MS.[2]: ground MS. ¶ 415 disproportions MS.[2]: gross disproportions MS: flagrant disproportions MS. *A.* ¶ 418 in a Vale MS.: by the side of this Lake MS. *A.* celebrity. MS.[2]: celebrity in MS. ¶ 419 Esthwaite MS.[2]: this Lake and MS. ¶ 420 lake MS.[2]: water MS. ¶ 420 it MS.[2]: this Lake MS. *After* it MS. *deletes*: of that *After* nature MS. *A deletes*: The traveller by A.side will not fail to ¶ 422 crystalline *Edd.*: christeline MS.* ¶ 423 No MS.[2]: The MS. ¶ 424 *After* materials MS. *deletes*: [equals *del.*] is not less fine [*altered to* fineness] than that which is woven for the ample [*blank*] of Windermere or Loch Lomond ¶ 425 sunshine MS.[2]: sun MS. ¶ 426 the stately breast of MS.[2]: the breast of the most stately Waters MS. ¶ 427 resort MS.[2]: come MS. ¶ 428 in winter MS.[2]: to enliven it in winter MS. Swallows MS.[2]: wheeling Swallows [which *del.*] that in summer MS. ¶ 429 the Boats MS.[2]: the few boats MS. *A.* ¶ 431 *After* which MS. *A deletes*: draw the inhabitants of.

Imagine to yourself the change which the variegated scene in front of which we are now resting undergoes when the abstractions of twilight have begun to take place among its forms, & when its colours retire before the shadows of approaching night; those numerous hills, which we now behold rising side by side & above each other on the opposite shore, pass gradually away from the sight till at length, with their cottages & fields & single trees, they have departed altogether, and the whole tract of ground assumes the appearance of one uniform mass, black & steep as a wall, insurmountable & uninhabitable. Above the summit, large clouds are perhaps poised in the firmament, with openings in them thro' which a radiance overshooting the gloom projected from the precipice finds its way to the still bosom of the lake.

Mid the dark steep's repose the shadowy streams,
As touch'd with dawning moonlight['s] hoary gleams
Where'er the faint breeze is stirring on the deep,
Soft o'er the surface the pale lustres creep
Pursuing & pursued; at once the bright
Gains on the shade, the shade upon the light.
Fair Spirits are abroad in sportive chase
Brushing with lucid wands the Water's face,
Wide field of calm delight in which they frame
The pensive measures of a noiseless game.

432 change MS.^{2}: appearance of MS.: appearance of the scene MS. *A.* variegated MS.^{2}: many featured MS. in front of MS.^{2}: near MS. ¶ 433 resting MS., MS. *A*^{2}: resting at the approach of twilight MS. *A.* ¶ 434 have begun MS.^{2}: are beginning MS. among its forms MS., MS. *A*^{2}: upon it MS. *A.* its colours MS.: its gay & diversified coulours [*sic*] MS. *A.* retire MS.^{3}: are fading MS.: [? retiring] MS.^{2}: are subdued by [?] shadows MS. *A.* ¶ 436 we now behold MS.^{2}: we have described as MS. ¶ 437 gradually MS.^{2}: imperceptibly MS. ¶ 438 departed altogether MS.^{2}: disappeared altogether MS.: wholly disappeared MS. *A.* ¶ 439–40 the whole ... mass, black MS.^{2}: the whole becomes [to the eye MS. *A*] one gloomy mass [black MS. *A*] steep MS., MS. *A.* ¶ 441 summit MS.^{2}: summit of this gloomy precipice MS. ¶ 445 streams MS.^{2}: gleams MS. ¶ 446 with dawning MS.^{2}: with hoary MS. moonlight's *Edd.*: moonlight MS. ¶ 449 Pursuing & pursued MS.^{3}: 'Tis restless magic all MS.: with [*blank*] interchange MS.^{2}.

At the entrance of the Village of Sawrey, we take our leave of the Vale of Esthwaite, but first looking back, we see the Langdale Pikes towering above the intervening hills, more conspicuous than before & in connection with a more splendid plain of Water, but the Town & Church of Hawkshead are now hidden from the view. In justice to this Vale I must say that of all approaches to it that from Coniston is the worst; we entered upon it cross wise & fronting the tame ridge, which forms its eastern boundary; and pursuing our way by the Lake side, if we had not looked back, we must have missed the most interesting combinations of scenery. Approached lengthways either from Ambleside on the North or from the South by either side of the lake, the Vale of Hawkshead wants neither beauty nor dignity. They who may have time will be repaid by making the Tour of the Lake; it is seen to advantage from the top of a small hill, over which the road passes about a ¼ of a mile from Hawkshead on the side opposite to that which we have taken; & when the last farm house on that side of the Vale is reached, it would be well to ascend some height the road which there branches off toward Ulverstone. The Lake from both these points is boldly broken by its peninsulas; the former view is well closed by Gommer's How, a [? communicating] Fell that rises from the farther shore of Windermere, & the latter by the capacious [? bosom] of Rydale head.

456 but MS.[2]: & here MS. ¶ 457 towering MS.[2]: still towering MS. conspicuous MS.[2]: conspicuously MS. ¶ 460 Coniston MS.[2]: Coniston along which our road has led us MS. ¶ 463 missed MS.[2]: lost MS. ¶ 465 South MS.[2]: Ferry house at Windermere on the MS. ¶ 466 Hawkshead wants ... dignity] MS.[2] *deletes but makes no substitution*: Hawkshead appears [?] MS. They MS.[2]: It is a MS. ¶ 467 *After* Lake MS. *deletes*: & upon reconsideration I do not scruple to advise those ¶ 468 over MS.[3]: on the MS.: about MS.[2]. ¶ 472 toward MS.[2]: to [*undel.*] MS. both MS.[2]: this MS. ¶ 474 *After* How MS. *deletes*: which Mountain rises from the: belonging to the eastern bank communicating] *G. W. reads*: considerable rises MS.[2]: makes [?] MS.*

THE SUBLIME & THE BEAUTIFUL

... amongst them. It is not likely that a person so situated, provided his imagination be exercised by other intercourse, as it ought to be, will become, by any continuance of familiarity, insensible to sublime impressions from the scenes around him. Nay, it is certain that his conceptions of the sublime, far from being dulled or narrowed by commonness or frequency, will be rendered more lively *&* comprehensive by more accurate observation and by encreasing knowledge. Yet, tho' this effect will take place with respect to grandeur, it will be much more strikingly felt in the influences of beauty. Neither the immediate nor final cause of this need here be examined; yet we may observe that, though it is impossible that a mind can be in a healthy state that is not frequently and strongly moved both by sublimity and beauty, it is more dependent for its daily well-being upon the love *&* gentleness which accompany the one, than upon the exaltation or awe which are created by the other. — Hence, as we advance in life, we can escape upon the invitation of our more placid *&* gentle nature from those obtrusive qualities in an object sublime in its general character; which qualities, at an earlier age, precluded imperiously the perception of beauty which that object if contemplated under another relation would have been capable of imparting. I need not observe to persons at all conversant in these speculations that I take for granted that the same object may be both sublime *&* beautiful; or, speaking more accurately, that it may have the power of affecting us both with the sense of beauty *&* the sense of sublimity; tho' (as for such Readers I need not add) the mind cannot be affected by both these sensations at the same time, for they are not only different from, but opposite to, each

131 them. MS.[2]: them *&* [? hence] [? the *or* ? tho] MS. ¶ 132 be exercised MS.[2], *Edd.*: be cultivated MS.: have been exercised MS.[3]. ¶ 135 far ... dulled MS.[3]: so far from dulling his pleasure [sensibility MS.[2]] MS. ¶ 136 will MS.[2]; it will MS. *An insertion above the deletion may be conjecturally read*: as the health [?] every kind is ¶ 138–39 will ... beauty MS.[2]: is in beauty MS. ¶ 139 beauty MS.[2]: beauty upon his mind MS. ¶ 143 well-being *Edd.*: welfare MS.: wel-being MS.[2]. ¶ 145 life MS.[2]: life those more obvious featur MS. ¶ 147 which qualities at an earlier age [ex MS.[3]] precluded imperiously the MS.[4]: which may have [prevented MS.] excluded the MS.[2]. ¶ 148 which that object ... been MS.[2]: which if contemplated under another relation it is MS. ¶ 151 the same MS.[2]: an MS. ¶ 155 time, for *Edd.*: time for, MS.

other. Now a Person unfamiliar with the appearances of a Mountainous Country is, with respect to its more conspicuous sublime features, in a situation resembling that of a Man of mature years when he looked upon such objects with the eye of childhood or youth. There appears to be something ungracious in this observation; yet it is nevertheless true, & the fact is mentioned both for its connection with the present work & for the importance of the general truth. Sensations of beauty & sublimity impress us very early in life; nor is it easy to determine which have precedence in point of time, & to which the sensibility of the mind in its natural constitution is more alive. But it may be confidently affirmed that, where the beautiful & the sublime co-exist in the same object, if that object be new to us, the sublime always precedes the beautiful in making us conscious of its presence — but all this may be both tedious & uninstructive to the Reader, as I have not explained what I mean by either of the words *sublime* or *beautiful*; nor is this the place to enter into a general disquisition upon the subject, or to attempt to clear away the errors by which it has been clouded. — But as I am persuaded that it is of infinite importance to the noblest feelings of the Mind & to its very highest powers that the forms of Nature should be accurately contemplated, &, if described, described in language that shall prove that we understand the several grand constitutional laws under which it has been ordained that these objects should everlastingly affect the mind, I shall deem myself justified in calling the Reader, upon the present humble occasion, to attend to a few words which shall be said upon two of these principal laws: the law of sublimity & that of beauty. These shall be considered so far at least as they may be collected from the objects amongst which we are

---

156 other. Now MS.[2]: other. The primary element in the sense of beauty is a distinct perception of parts MS. Person MS.[2]: Stranger MS. ⸿ 156 unfamiliar MS.[3]: unf MS.: who MS.[2]. is, with MS.[3]: stands MS.: is in MS.[2]. ⸿ 158 of a Man MS.[3]: of a child MS.: in which MS.[2]. ⸿ 162 truth] *Possibly* truths *as originally written; the downward stroke at the end of the word may be either part of the s or a mark of deletion.** ⸿ 170 into *Edd.*: upon into MS. ⸿ 173 noblest ... Mind MS.[2]: the mind MS. ⸿ 175 described, MS.[2]: described in appropriate lang MS. ⸿ 177 deem *Edd.*: deemed MS. ⸿ 180–81 so far at least as MS.[3]: so far as MS.: not in so far MS.[2].

about to enter, viz., those of a mountainous region — and to begin with the sublime as it exists in such landscape.

Let me then invite the Reader to turn his eyes with me towards that cluster of Mountains at the Head of Windermere; it is probable that they will settle ere long upon the Pikes of Langdale & the black precipice contiguous to them. — If these objects be so distant that, while we look at them, they are only thought of as the crown of a comprehensive Landscape; if our minds be not perverted by false theories, unless those mountains be seen under some accidents of nature, we shall receive from them a grand impression, and nothing more. But if they be looked at from a point which has brought us so near that the mountain is almost the sole object before our eyes, yet not so near but that the whole of it is visible, we shall be impressed with a sensation of sublimity. — And if this is analyzed, the body of this sensation would be found to resolve itself into three component parts: a sense of individual form or forms; a sense of duration; and a sense of power. The whole complex impression is made up of these elementary parts, & the effect depends upon their co-existence. For, if any one of them were abstracted, the others would be deprived of their power to affect.

I first enumerated individuality of form; this individual form was then invested with qualities and powers, ending with duration. Duration is evidently an element of the sublime; but think of it without reference to individual form, and we shall perceive that it has no power to affect the mind. Cast your eye, for example, upon any commonplace ridge or eminence that cannot be separated, without some effort of the mind, from the general mass of the planet; you may be persuaded, nay, convinced, that it has borne that shape as long as or longer than Cader Idris,

185–86 it … they MS.^{2}: they MS. ℂ 191 receive MS.^{2}: pro[?] receive MS. ℂ 194 visible, *Edd.*: visible: if this be analyzed MS: visible: MS.^{2}. ℂ 195 And if this is MS.^{3}: This if MS.: and if this were MS.^{2}. would MS.^{2}: will MS. ℂ 196 three MS.^{2}: four MS. ℂ 197 *After* forms MS. *deletes*: — of motion, abrupt, rapid or precipitous as expressed by the [? lin *del.*] outlines of the mountain before us ℂ 201 individuality of form MS.^{2}: individual form MS. ℂ 208 than MS.^{2}: than the pikes MS. ℂ 208 Cader Idris *Edd.*: Caderideris MS.

or Snowdon, or the Pikes of Langdale that are before us; and the mind is wholly unmoved by the thought; and the only way in which such an object can affect us, contemplated under the notion of duration, is when the faint sense which we have of its individuality is lost in the general sense of duration belonging to the Earth itself. Prominent individual form must, therefore, be conjoined with duration, in order that Objects of this kind may impress a sense of sublimity; &, in the works of Man, this conjunction is, for obvious reasons, of itself sufficient for the purpose. But in works of Nature it is not so: with these must be combined impressions of power, to a sympathy with & a participation of which the mind must be elevated — or to a dread and awe of which, as existing out of itself, it must be subdued. A mountain being a stationary object is enabled to effect this in connection with duration and individual form, by the sense of motion which in the mind accompanies the lines by which the Mountain itself is shaped out. These lines may either be abrupt and precipitous, by which danger & sudden change is expressed; or they may flow into each other like the waves of the sea, &, by involving in such image a feeling of self-propagation infinitely continuous and without cognizable beginning, these lines may thus convey to the Mind sensations not less sublime than those which were excited by their opposites, the abrupt and the precipitous. And, to compleat this sense of power expressed by these permanent objects, add the torrents which take their rise within its bosom, & roll foaming down its sides;

212–13 in the general sense MS.[2]: under the feeling MS. ℂ 213 Prominent MS.[2]: [? to] MS. ℂ 214 conjoined MS.[2]: combined MS. ℂ 215 may impress a MS.[2]: must be conjoined to impress us with the MS. ℂ 215–16 & ... Man MS.[2]: but in the works of Nature MS. ℂ 217 with MS.[2]: but MS.* ℂ 220 subdued MS.[2]: [? drea]-ded MS. ℂ 220–21 A mountain ... this in MS.[2]: A stationary object as a mountain is, is enabled to MS. ℂ 224 danger & sudden change is MS.[2]: sudden danger is MS. ℂ 227 beginning MS.[2]: beginning or termination MS. ℂ 228 to the Mind sensations not less MS.[2]: to the Mind by these causes sensations which are the reverse of [? this as] MS.** ℂ 231 sides; *Edd.*: sides, MS. it attracts MS.[2]: gather round it MS.

the clouds which it attracts; the stature with which it appears to reach the sky; the storms with which it arms itself; the triumphant ostentation with which its snows defy the sun, &c.

Thus has been given an analysis of the attributes or qualities the co-existence of which gives to a Mountain the power of affecting the mind with a sensation of sublimity. The capability of perceiving these qualities, & the degree in which they are perceived, will of course depend upon the state or condition of the mind, with respect to habits, knowledge, & powers, which is brought within the reach of their influence. It is to be remembered that I have been speaking of a visible object; & it might seem that when I required duration to be combined with individual form, more was required than was necessary; for a native of a mountainous country, looking back upon his childhood, will remember how frequently he has been impressed by a sensation of sublimity from a precipice, in which awe or personal apprehension were the predominant feelings of his mind, & from which the milder influence of duration seemed to be excluded. And it is true that the relative proportions in which we are affected by the qualities of these objects are different at different periods of our lives; yet there cannot be a doubt that upon all ages they act conjointly. The precipitous form of an individual cloud which a Child has been taught by tales & pictures to think of as sufficiently solid to support a substantial body, & upon which he finds it easy to conceive himself as seated, in imagination, and thus to invest it with some portion of the terror which belongs to the precipice, would affect him very languidly, &, surely, much more from the knowledge which he has of its evanescence than from the less degree in which it excites in him feelings of dread. Familiarity with these objects tends very much to mitigate & to destroy the power which they have to produce the sensation of sublimity

---

232–33 the clouds ... the triumphant *Edd.*: by the clouds ... by the stature ... by the storms ... by the triumphant MS. ❨ 233 sky; *Edd.*: sky — MS.* ❨ 235 qualities MS.[2]: qualities by which MS. ❨ 237 capability MS.[2]: power MS. ❨ 241 object; *Edd.*: object, MS. ❨ 247 from MS.[2]: [? on *or* in] MS. ❨ 248 excluded. And *Edd.*: excluded & MS. ❨ 249 different [*first*] MS.[2]: very different MS. ❨ 253 he finds it easy MS.[2]: it [? seems] [? easy] MS.

as dependent upon personal fear or upon wonder; a comprehensive awe takes the place of the one, and a religious admiration of the other, & the condition of the mind is exalted accordingly. — Yet it cannot be doubted that a Child or an unpracticed person whose mind is possessed by the sight of a lofty precipice, with its attire of hanging rocks & starting trees, &c., has been visited by a sense of sublimity, if personal fear & surprize or wonder have not been carried beyond certain bounds. For whatever suspends the comparing power of the mind & possesses it with a feeling or image of intense unity, without a conscious contemplation of parts, has produced that state of the mind which is the consummation of the sublime. — But if personal fear be strained beyond a certain point, this sensation is destroyed, for there are two ideas that divide & distract the attention of the Spectator with an accompanying repulsion or a wish in the soul [that] they should be divided: the object exciting the fear & the subject in which it is excited. And this leads me to a remark which will remove the main difficulties of this investigation. Power awakens the sublime either when it rouses us to a sympathetic energy & calls upon the mind to grasp at something towards which it can make approaches but which it is incapable of attaining — yet so that it participates force which is acting upon it; or, 2dly, by producing a humiliation or prostration of the mind before some external agency which it presumes not to make an effort to participate, but is absorbed in the contemplation of the might in the external power, &, as far as it has any consciousness of itself, its grandeur subsists in the naked fact of being conscious of external Power at once awful & immeasurable; so that, in both cases, the head & the front of the sensation is intense unity. But if that Power which is exalted above our sympathy impresses the

260 as dependent upon MS.^{2}; by MS. ¶ 260 upon [*second*] MS.^{2}: by MS. ¶ 265 if MS.^{2}: [? then] MS. ¶ 267 power] *possibly* powers. ¶ 271 ideas MS.^{2}: objects MS. ¶ 272 with an MS.^{3}, MS.: by MS.^{2}. or MS.^{2}: [? with] MS. ¶ 273 that *Edd.*: *om.* MS. ¶ 275 of MS.^{2}: which have hung around this subject MS. ¶ 279 force MS.^{2}; [? that] power MS. ¶ 283–84 the naked ... conscious MS.^{2}: being capable MS. ¶ 284 Power MS.^{2}; Power so [? aw] MS. ¶ 286 if MS.^{2}: when MS. impresses MS.^{3}: has impressed MS.; should be thought of as having MS.^{2}.

mind with personal fear, so as the sensation becomes more lively than the impression or thought of the exciting cause, then self-consideration & all its accompanying littleness takes place of the sublime, & wholly excludes it. Or if the object contemplated be of a spiritual nature, as that of the Supreme Being, for instance (though few minds, I will hope, are so far degraded that with reference to the Deity they can be affected by sensations of personal fear, such as a precipice, a conflagration, a torrent, or a shipwreck might excite), yet it may be confidently affirmed that no sublimity can be raised by the contemplation of such power when it presses upon us with pain and individual fear to a degree which takes precedence in our thoughts [over] the power itself. For connect with such sensations the notion of infinity, or any other ideas of a sublime nature which different religious sects have connected with it: the feeling of self being still predominant, the condition of the mind would be mean & abject. — Accordingly Belial, the most sensual spirit of the fallen Angels, tho' speaking of himself & his Companions as full of pain, yet adds:

Who would lose those thoughts
Which wander thro' Eternity?

The thoughts are not chained down by anguish, but they are free, and tolerate neither limit nor circumscription. Though by the opinions of many religious sects, not less than by many other examples, it is lamentably shewn how industrious Man is in perverting & degrading his mind, yet such is its inherent dignity that, like that of the fallen Spirit as exhibited by the Philosophic & religious Poet, he is perpetually thwarted & baffled & rescued in his own despite.

But to return: Whence comes it, then, that that external power, to a union or communion with which we feel that we can make no approxi-

295 raised MS.[2]: excited MS. ℂ 297 precedence in our thoughts MS.[2]; precedence [? for] MS. over *Edd.*: over *is perhaps written on top of the smeared deletion.* ℂ 298 the notion of infinity MS.[2]: of infinity [? to] MS. ℂ 299 it MS.[2]: them MS. the feeling of self being MS.[2]; as the feeling of self is MS. ℂ 308 tolerate MS.[2]: admit MS. neither limit MS.[2]; no limit to their MS. Though MS.[2]: Though Man has been MS.

mation while it produces humiliation & submission, reverence or adoration, & all those sensations which may be denominated passive, does nevertheless place the mind in a state that is truly sublime? As I have said before, this is done by the notion or image of intense unity, with which the Soul is occupied or possessed. — But how is this produced or supported, &, when it remits, & the mind is distinctly conscious of his own being & existence, whence comes it that it willingly & naturally relapses into the same state? The cause of this is either that our physical nature has only to a certain degree been endangered, or that our moral Nature has not in the least degree been violated. — The point beyond which apprehensions for our physical nature consistent with sublimity may be carried, has been ascertained; &, with respect to power acting upon our moral or spiritual nature, by awakening energy either that would resist or that [? hopes] to participate, the sublime is called forth. But if the Power contemplated be of that kind which neither admits of the notion of resistance or participation, then it may be confidently said that, unless the apprehensions which it excites terminate in repose, there can be no sublimity, & that this sense of repose is the result of reason & the moral law. Could this be abstracted & the reliance upon it taken away, no species of Power that was absolute over the mind could beget a sublime sensation; but, on the contrary, it could never be thought of without fear and degradation.

I have been seduced to treat the subject more generally than I had at first proposed; if I have been so fortunate as to make myself understood, what has been said will be forgiven. Let us now contract the speculation, & confine it to the sublime as it exists in a mountainous Country, & to the manner in which it makes itself felt. I enumerated the qualities which must be perceived in a Mountain before a sense of sublimity can

---

316 or MS.[2]: & MS. ¶ 319 the notion MS.[2]: the intense MS. ¶ 320 But MS.[2]: but when this remits & the consciousness MS. ¶ 323 either that MS.[2]: that MS. ¶ 325–26 beyond which MS.[3]: [?] in [of MS.[2]] which MS. ¶ 326 *After* nature MS. *deletes*: may be [? ascer]tained ¶ 327 to power MS.[2]: to our m MS. ¶ 342 enumerated *Edd.*: ennumerated MS. ¶ 343 perceived MS.[2]: recognized MS.

be received from it. Individuality of form is the primary requisite; and the form must be of that character that deeply impresses the sense of power. And power produces the sublime either as it is thought of as a thing to be dreaded, to be resisted, or that can be participated. To what degree consistent with sublimity power may be dreaded has been ascertained; but as power, contemplated as something to be opposed or resisted, implies a twofold agency of which the mind is conscious, this state seems to be irreconcilable to what has been said concerning the consummation of sublimity, which, as has been determined, exists in the extinction of the comparing power of the mind, & in intense unity. But the fact is, there is no sublimity excited by the contemplation of power thought of as a thing to be resisted & which the moral law enjoins us to resist, saving only as far as the mind, either by glances or continuously, conceives that that power may be overcome or rendered evanescent, and as far as it feels itself tending towards the unity that exists in security or absolute triumph. — (When power is thought of under a mode which we can & do participate, the sublime sensation consists in a manifest ap[p]roximation towards absolute unity.) If the resistance contemplated be of a passive nature (such, for example, as the Rock in the middle of the fall of the Rhine at Chafhausen, as opposed for countless ages to that mighty mass of Waters), there are undoubtedly here before us two distinct images & thoughts; & there is a most complex instrumentality acting upon the senses, such as the roar of the Water, the fury of the foam, &c.; and an instrumentality still more comprehensive, furnished by the imagination, and drawn from the length of the River's course,

---

344 Individuality MS.[2]: Before MS. ¶ 346 power. MS.[2]: power either to MS. ¶ 347 thing MS.[2]: thing either MS. or that *Edd.*: or to that MS. ¶ 349 contemplated MS.[2]: to be resisted MS. ¶ 349–50 as something ... implies MS.[3]: as [opposed & resisted MS.[2]] something to be resisted it might seem that the notion of resistance implies MS. ¶ 350 agency MS.[3]: agency it should seem MS.: agency it seems MS.[2]. ¶ 351 what MS.[2]: that which MS. ¶ 354–55 power ... to be MS.[2]: power that may be MS. ¶ 359 *After* triumph MS. *deletes*: — It therefore appears that in which under a mode MS.[2]: as a thing MS. ¶ 366 acting MS.[2]: employed MS. ¶ 367 and ... comprehensive MS.[2]: & a still more comprehensive MS.

the Mountains from which it rises, the various countries thro' which it flows, & the distant Seas in which its waters are lost. These images & thoughts will, in such a place, be present to the mind, either personally or by representative abstractions more or less vivid. — Yet to return to the rock & the Waterfall: these objects will be found to have exalted the mind to the highest state of sublimity when they are thought of in that state of opposition & yet reconcilement, analogous to parallel lines in mathematics, which, being infinitely prolonged, can never come nearer to each other; & hence, tho' the images & feelings above enumerated have exerted a preparative influence upon the mind, the absolute crown of the impression is infinity, which is a modification of unity.

Having had the image of a mighty River before us, I cannot but, in connection with it, observe that the main source of all the difficulties & errors which have attended these disquisitions is that the attention of those who have been engaged in them has been primarily & chiefly fixed upon external objects & their powers, qualities, & properties, & not upon the mind itself, & the laws by which it is acted upon. Hence the endless disputes about the characters of objects, and the absolute denial on the part of many that sublimity or beauty exists. To talk of an object as being sublime or beautiful in itself, without references to some subject by whom that sublimity or beauty is perceived, is absurd; nor is it of the slightest importance to mankind whether there be any object with which their minds are conversant that Men would universally agree (after having ascertained that the words were used in the same sense) to denominate sublime or beautiful. It is enough that there are, both in moral qualities & in the forms of the external universe, such qualities & powers as have affected Men, in different states of civilization & without communication with each other, with similar sensations either of the sublime or beautiful. The true province of the philosopher is not to

379 *After* unity. MS. *deletes*: Lastly when power is thought of under a mode ℂ 387 To talk of MS.[2]: It is a matter of no importance whether there be in Nature MS. ℂ 391 with which *Edd.*: which which MS. Men MS.[2]: they MS. ℂ 395 as have affected MS.[2]: as have the power of comp MS. ℂ 395 civilization MS.[2]: civilization with similar MS.

grope about in the external world &, when he has perceived or detected in an object such or such a quality or power, to set himself to the task of persuading the world that such is a sublime or beautiful object, but to look into his own mind & determine the law by which he is affected. — He will then find that the same object has power to affect him in various manners at different times; so that, ludicrous as it [......] to power as governed some where by the intelligence of law & reason, and lastly to the transcendent sympathies which have been vouchsafed to her with the calmness of eternity.

Thus, then, is apparent how various are the *means* by which we are conducted to the same end — the elevation of our being; & the practical influences to be drawn from this are most important, but I shall consider them only with reference to the forms of nature which have occasioned this disquisition.

I have already given a faint sketch of the manner in which a familiarity with these objects acts upon the minds of men of cultivated imagination. I will now suppose a person of mature age to be introduced amongst them for the first time. I will not imagine him to be a man particularly conversant with pictures, nor an enthusiast in poetry; but he shall be modest & unpresumptuous, one who has not been insensible to impressions of grandeur from the universal or less local appearances & forms of nature (such as the sky, the clouds, the heavenly bodies, rivers, trees, & perhaps the Ocean), & coming hither desirous to have his knowledge increased & the means of exalting himself in thought & feeling multiplied & extended. I can easily conceive that such a man, in his first intercourse with these objects, might be grievously disappointed, &,

---

399 object MS.^{2}: object or quality MS. ¶ 403 so that MS.^{2}: so that the [? might] MS. ¶ 403 *Page* [7^{v}] *of* MS. Prose 28^{b}, *which the* MS. *numbers* 14, *ends at* ludicrous as it; *page* [8^{r}] *is numbered* 17 *and begins* to power as governed. *Presumably a loose quarter sheet, numbered* 15 *on the recto and* 16 *on the verso, was once here inserted and has since been lost.* ¶ 405 which *Edd.*: which which MS. ¶ 409 this MS.^{2}: this as applicable to MS. ¶ 417 shall MS.^{2}: shall nevertheless MS. modest MS.^{2}; a Man of candour MS. *After* unpresumptuous MS. *deletes*: willing & wishing to be pleased & desirous to have his mind opened out & exalted ¶ 421 knowledge MS.^{2}: mind MS. increased MS.^{2}: extended MS. in MS.^{2}: into MS. ¶ 423 might MS.^{2}: should MS.

if that intercourse should be short, might depart without being raised from that depression which such disappointment might reasonably cause. Such would have been the condition of the most eminent of our English Painters if his visits to the sublime pictures in the Vatican & the Cistine Chapel had not been repeated till the sense of strangeness had worn off, till the twilight of novelty began to dispel, and he was made conscious of the mighty difference between seeing & perceiving. I have heard of a Lady, a native of the Orcades (which naked solitudes from her birth she had never quitted), whose imagination, endeavouring to compleat whatever had been left imperfect in pictures & books, had feasted in representing to itself the forms of trees. With delight did she look forward to the day when it would be permitted to her to behold the reality, & to learn by experience how far its grandeur or beauty surpassed the conceptions which she had formed — but sad & heavy was her disappointment when this wish was satisfied. A journey to a fertile Vale in the South of Scotland gave her an opportunity of seeing some of the finest trees in the Island; but she beheld them without pleasure or emotion, & complained that, compared with the grandeur of the living & ever-varying ocean in all the changes & appearances & powers of which she was thoroughly versed — that a tree or a wood were objects insipid and lifeless. — Something of a like disappointment, or perhaps a kind of blank & stupid wonder (one of the most oppressive of sensations), might be felt by one who had passed his life in the plains of Lincolnshire & should be suddenly transported to the recesses of Borrowdale or Glencoe. And if this feeling should not burthen his mind, innumerable are

---

429 and he was MS.[2]: & the veil was uplifted by which MS. ℂ 430 *After* perceiving MS. *deletes*: [?] are the associations which MS.[2]: who in those MS. ℂ 431 solitudes from MS.[3]: solitudes beyond the limits she had MS.: solitudes which MS.[2]. ℂ 432 whose imagination MS.[3]: who had feasted her imagination [& MS.[2]] in MS. ℂ 434 *After* trees MS. *deletes*: & in connecting with those pictures of her mind completing whatever had been left imperfect by pictures & books to bring (*Wordsworth's hand writes* completing ... bring). ℂ 438 *After* satisfied MS. *deletes*: she had an opportunity some of [*sic*] the finest trees in the Island upon ℂ 442 in MS.[2]: with MS. ℂ 443 tree or MS.[3]: tree & doubtless MS.: tree [?] MS.[2]. objects MS.[2]: an object MS. ℂ 447 recesses MS.[2]: plains MS. And MS.[2]: or MS.

the impressions which may exclude him from a communication with the sublime in the midst of objects eminently capable of exciting that feeling: he may be depressed by the image of barrenness; or the chaotic appearance of crags heaped together, or seemingly ready to fall upon each other, may excite in him sensations as uncomfortable as those with which he would look upon an edifice that the Builder had left unfinished; & many of the forms before his eyes, by associations of outward likeness, merely may recal [*sic*] to his mind mean or undignified works of art; & every where might he be haunted or disturbed by a sense of incongruity, either light & trivial, or resembling in kind that intermixture of the terrible & the ludicrous which dramatists who understand the constitution of the human mind have not unfrequently represented when they introduce a character disturbed by an agency supernatural or horrible to a degree beyond what the mind is prepared to expect from the ordinary course of human calamities or afflictions. So that it appears that even those impressions that do most easily make their way to the human mind, such as I deem those of the sublime to be, cannot be received from an object however eminently qualified to impart them, without a preparatory intercourse with that object or with others of the same kind.

But impediments arising merely from novelty or inexperience in a well disposed mind disappear gradually and assuredly. Yet, though it will not be long before the Stranger will become conscious of the sublime where the power to raise it eminently exists, yet, if I may judge from my own experience, it is only very slowly that the mind is opened out to a perception of images of Beauty co-existing in the same object with

449 with MS.[2]: of MS. ¶ 451 *After* barrenness MS. *deletes*: perplexed by a sense of confusion ¶ 452 together MS.[2]: upon each other MS. ¶ 455 *After* likeness MS. *deletes*: which [? I *or* h] ¶ 458 trivial MS.[2]: ludicrous MS. ¶ 458–59 that … dramatists MS.[2]: tho' in [? course] not in degree those which dramatists MS. ¶ 461 disturbed MS.[2]: affected MS. ¶ 462 prepared MS.[2]: thought MS. ¶ 464 impressions MS.[3]: sensations MS.: thoughts MS.[3].* ¶ 466–67 intercourse with MS.[3]: intercourse either with MS. object MS.[2]; class of objects MS. ¶ 468 inexperience MS.[2]: inexperience do MS. ¶ 470 Stranger MS.[2]: mind MS. ¶ 471 raise MS.[2]: excite MS.

those of sublimity. As I have explained at large what I mean by the word sublimity, I might with propriety here proceed to treat of beauty, & to explain in what manner I conceive the mind to be affected when it has a sense of the beautiful. But I cannot pass from the sublime without guarding the ingenuous reader against those caprices of vanity & presumption derived from false teachers in the philosophy of the fine arts & of taste, which Painters, connesieurs, & amateurs are perpetually interposing between the light of nature & their own minds. Powerful indeed must be the spells by which such an eclipse is to be removed; but nothing is wanting, save humility, modesty, diffidence, & an habitual, kindly, & confident communion with Nature, to prevent such a darkness from ever being superinduced. "Oh," says one of these tutored spectators, "what a scene should we have before us here upon the shores of Windermere, if we could but strike out those pikes of Langdale by which it is terminated; they are so intensely *picturesque* that their presence excludes from the mind all sense of the sublime." Extravagant as such an ejaculation is, it has been heard from the mouths of Persons who pass for intelligent men of cultivated mind.

474–75 As ... here MS.[3]: I might here with propriety MS.: As ... I might here with propriety MS.[2]. ¶ 476 explain MS.[2]; define MS. *After* affected MS. *deletes*: by an object which supposing us to speak ¶ 479 derived MS.[2]: which have been derived MS. in the MS.[2]: in the fine MS. philosophy *Edd.*: phylosophy MS. ¶ 480 which Painters ... are MS.[2]: with which artists Connesieurs & amateurs have narrowed MS. ¶ 481–82 Powerful ... spells MS.[2]: I know not by what spells MS. ¶ 482 is ... removed MS.[2]: may be removed MS. ¶ 484 with Nature MS.[2]: with & reliance upon Nature and MS. ¶ 485 tutored spectators MS.[3]: ripened connesieurs from MS.: ripened connesieurs, come on a visit to MS.[2]. scene MS.[2]: sublime scene MS. ¶ 487 out those *Edd.*: out of the land [scene MS.[2]] yon MS.: out of those MS.[3]. ¶ 488 they are so *Edd.*: they are peculiar & so MS.: they so MS.[2]. ¶ 490 been MS.[2]: been frequently MS. ¶ 490–91 Persons ... men MS.[2]: more than one Person who passes for an intelligent man MS.

ENDNOTES

*5. 22 *After* notice MS. *deletes*: Yet this [innocent perverseness *del.*] busy propensity of which numerous instances are extant in [these Valleys which *del.*] this [beautiful *del.*] Country [which Nature has <beautifully *del.*> framed so beautifully & prodigally *del.*] beautifully framed & prodigally adorned by nature. [Combined with *del.*] This and the perverseness with which the dwellings often turn their backs upon the most beautiful landscapes even where there is not the excuse of a little sunshine seems to shew that [the admiration of *del.*] though [indifference *del.*] insensibility or indifference to the [grand and beautiful productions & *del.*] general forms of nature does not exist in a state of society however rude that a relish for fine combinations of Landscapes is an acquired taste. So capacious is the human mind that it can find space for things widely separated from each other in spirit & character & a liking for these uncouth [? fancies] may consist with an admiration of the wild & careless graces of the woods & fields. *Cf. textual n.* 1179.

*7. 73 With those, therefore MS.^{2}: I may therefore claim credit with MS. *After* extent of *there occurs a heavily deleted passage, giving a first draft of* 22–25 (This waywardness ... Nature); *it may be conjecturally read*: This waywardness [? and] the [?] it is never the less in the spirit a step in the progress of refinement; a [?] link that connects man with the [?] nature By his own activity [? any man] in this connection, by a tie less gross than that of necessity has [?].

**7. 79–133 *At* 79 *the text of* MS. Prose 23^{b} *originally continued with the matter now given in* 133–211; *but* MS. Prose 23^{g}, *written as an afterthought, was clearly intended for insertion here, and accordingly* 80–132 *derives from* MS. Prose 23^{g} (*see our description of* MSS. Prose 23 *and see also textual n.* 132).

*8. *The top of page* [2^{r}] *of* MS. Prose 23^{g} *is torn down the centre for about* 2 *in. because* 98 *ff. was written after the tear occurred, nothing of the text was here lost. But before the tear occurred, the top of the page had been used for an early draft of* 440–43: [upon *del.*] where the summit of it [*tear*] large [*tear*] poized in the firmament with [*tear*] openings in them thro which [pale lights find their *del.*] a [?] finds its way to the still bosom of [the Lake *del.*]

*9. 127 *After* Thou knowest." MS. *deletes*: At that time the Minister of this congregation of Anabaptists used to preach once a month in a private House in

Langdale, a [labour that *del.*] must have been attended with great [? effects *or* efforts] [as he was zealous in the discharge of his duty & *del.*] as the place [which *del.*] stood in [? much] need of such attention [? As] the [?] benefits [of the established Church had scarcely been extended *del.*] [?] For though a Chapel of the Church of England existed there, the stipend not being more than five pounds per Annum, unless the Incumbent Clergyman [had *del.*] were a man of extraordinary character it was not likely that he would be competent to the discharge of his duty ℂ 129–132 a chearful salutation ... lead to] MS. *A gives numerous rewritings, almost all in Wordsworth's hand; without noting all the deletions, we record, in chronological order, some of these drafts*: a striking contrast to the obscure and forlorn House of Worship which we have left. At the foot of the hill within half a mile of Hawkshead a [?] embowering in trees and opposite to an antient Building [*cf. textual n.* 132]: a chearing sight particularly to those who may be occupied by serious reflexions: may have turned aside to visit the [?] & baptismal reservoir belonging to this forlorn House of Worship: & whose minds are occupied with such serious reflexions as those images will naturally lead to: a chearful salutation particularly as it is scarcely possible to have: A chearful salutation & particularly so for those whose minds it may relieve from such serious reflections as the [forlorn *del.*] obscure House of Worship & its appurtenances which we have left naturally lead to. ℂ 132 *After* lead to. *Wordsworth's hand immediately writes (we omit the deletions)*: At the foot of the hill pleasantly [? embowered] in trees stands an antient Building *This continuation clearly marks the end of the insertion and leads us back to* 79, *or* MS. Prose 23[b], *where the text reads*: ... Vale of Conistone [. Nothing remarkable occurs till we come *del.*] we have left. At the foot of the hill within ½ mile of Hawkshead [where we may notice on the left an ancient *del.*] stands by the road side an ancient Building [*cf.* 133–35].

**9. 140–150 MS. Prose 23[f], *written as an afterthought, contains matter apparently intended for insertion somewhere around here, but unlike* 80–132, *it was never worked into the text. Because the final version, which we give first, is a long one, we will punctuate it, as we normally punctuate other U.T. manuscripts*: The situation of Hawkshead is excellent but its aspect, notwithstanding, from this quarter is far from agreeable. How much grace might not towns of this compass easily derive from a few trees intermingled with the houses, softening the glare of whitewashed walls & connecting the smoke which ascends from the chimneys with soothing images of rural seclusion & quietness! But this little Town, as we [approach it from this *del.*] are approaching it, appears a mere accumulation of naked buildings, unfurnished even with gardens to unite it with the country. The Church, also in itself a pleasing object happily placed, has within these few years been strangely disfigured by the erection of a Vestry, the roof of which runs in a line with the lower roof of the Church. This excrescence cuts off the lower base of the Steeple so that all the lightness which that part of the structure possessed [has been *del.*], as being in shape [for *del.*] distinctly separated from the body of the Church, is destroyed, nor has pains been taken to make the window uniform with those of the Church that run in a line with it. In a book of this kind one chief purpose of which is by commenting upon the face of the Country, as we pass along it, to endeavour to preserve its natural beauty & [establishing *del.*] to establish at the same time principals of taste which may extend their influence beyond the district which furnished the occasion for illustrating them, this notice will not be deemed insignificant, especially by those who feel a debt of gratitude to our ancestors for the rich inheritance of sacred architure [*sic*] which they have [transmitted MS. *A*, *Edd.*: *om.* MS.] to us. Besides it is difficult not to apprehend that there may be a decay of piety among those who when alterations & additions are called for in [such *del.*] structures raised with munificence & nice attention, execute them so carelessly, or in so mean & discordant a style as shews that the [chief thing aimed at *del.*] point most attended to was saving of expence. [In truth *del.*] We may confidently affirm none of the fine arts — if Poetry be excepted which is a spirit in the mind, a thing sui generis — have so much pleasurable & even valuable feeling dependent upon them as architecture. There is not a building, however [low *del.*] vulgar the purposes to which it may be applied, that will not admit of being constructed according to proportions [from *del.*] [by *del.*] which the mind may receive [delight *del.*] a [*? del.*] which [gratifies *del.*] These pleasures also are a free gift, presented to us without search in all moods and upon all occasions; and [on the contrary *del.*] in like manner, which further [proves *del.*] shews the comparative importance of architecture, the disgust which its productions excite, if bad, cannot be escaped. [In fact *del.*] In the present state of this art, it is painful to think how much the [pleasures *del.*] encouragements of a new taste in the Country lie at the mercy of the builder. There [There is *del.*] This dignity also belongs to Architecture: that it is not an imitative art, but a necessary appendage to human existence, that its works are incorporated with those of Nature, & that there is no combination of her forms the beauty or grandeur of which may not be heightened by [*the remaining text is uncertain*] the presence of some edifice subservient to the safety, the comfort of men, or [expressing *del.*] telling with sublimity or lowliness his dependence on his Maker, his hope, & his consolation.

An earlier version, also in the hand of Mary Wordsworth, reads: The situation of this little town is excellent but its appearance notwithstanding from this quarter is [unattractive *del.*] far from agreeable it is a mere accumulation of naked [houses *del.*] buildings no gardens unite it with the Country [no *del.*] [*?* for] a few trees intermingling with the houses soften the glare of the White washed fronts walls [*sic*] or break the horizontal line of their roofs or connect the smoke which ascends from the Chimneys with soothing images of rural seclusion & quietness The Church also in itself a pleasing object happily placed has been within these few years strangely disfigured by the erection of a Vestry the roof of which runs in a line with the lower roof of the Church cutting off the base of the Steeple so that all the lightness which that part of the structure possessed as being in shape distinctly separated from top to bottom of the body of the Church is destroyed nor has pains been taken to make the window of this excrescence uniform with those of the Church which run in a line with it In a [work *del.*] Book of this kind [these observations will one of the main purposes of which is to comment upon the face of the Country <? wh> are *del.*] one of the chief purposes of which is by commenting upon the face of the Country as we pass along [with a view to prevent <?> *del.*] to save it from being further disfigured & to establish principles of taste which may extend their influence beyond the district which furnishes the present occasion for illustrating them these [observations *del.*] notices will not [appear too minute *del.*] be deemed insignificant especially to those [who with the Author may rank architecture place architecture with the first rank of the fine arts *del.*]

A first draft contains mainly disconnected and repetitious bits: but thought of gratitude ... we remember [? how] much we are indebted to our [fathers *del.*] ancestors for the rich inheritance of sacred Architecture [to which both in Town & in village *del.*] which they have transmitted to us. A want of taste is certainly shown & it is difficult not to apprehend ... None of the fine arts are so important as Architecture [its productions are *del.*] there is not a building before us at all seasons Numerous are the purposes to which it is applied [?] will not admit of being constructed according to proportions ... at once [gratify *del.*] please their eye & their Intellect The productions of this art are everywhere exposed to us and unless ... In the Country they are incorporated with the work of Nature ... None of the fine arts have so much pleasurable & even valuable feeling dependent upon them as architecture and none are so imperfect Their encouragements which to men of taste may lie almost at the mercy of this Art. There is not a building however mean the purpose for which it [? may] be applied that will not admit of being constructed according to proposes [*sic*] that will [not equally *del.*] delight the mind.

***9. 144 *After* Hawkshead MS. *deletes*: [which presides over it with its *del.*] seated under a hill upon the top of which stands a handsome Church having a tower and double roof and making an object that with sufficient dignity presides over this short & narrow Vale. Immediately Under [the Church *del.*] the hill on the eastern side of the Church stands the School-house founded & liberally endowed by archbishop Sandes a Native of this neighbourhood.

*12. 206–09 Upon a ... maneuvering MS.[3]: From this seat upon a summer afternoon [when the shadows of the clouds are deep and determined MS.[2]] the fells of Kirkstone & Rydale head often look like a vast tract of chosen ground upon which detachments of a silent army of sunbeams & shadows are maneuvering MS.

**12. 220 sacred MS.: *not in* MS. *A. After* Smith MS. *A deletes*: a young Person of admirable accomplishments, and acquisitions [*?* &] learning not [*?*] who died a few years ago at [*?* Newl *del.*] Conistone [her father's <residence *del.*> house in <*?*> It is generally known that a reverse in fortune compelled this family to quit their <residence *del.*> abode upon the banks of the Wye & the regret which in <*?*> This painful oc <*?*> <*?* sacrificed> in relinquishing <*?*> of that MS. *A*[2]] & was buried here That regret which a mind [so *del.*] tenderly alive to the beautiful in every thing must have felt in being compelled to quit the family residence on the banks of the Wye was in course of time alleviated by [an opportunity *del.*] new attachments to scenes of Nature still more beautiful & sublime which her residence in this Country gave her an opportunity of forming — to the strength of these attachments [she *del.*] this lamented young woman gave in her last illness a most affecting testimony — it is recorded that, when in a state of threatening debility she was inhaling the fresh air within a tent placed upon a knoll by the side of Coniston Water & [the conversation <*?* turned> upon the <*?* propriety>] [the <*?* trial> of a milder climate was recommended to her &] for the restoration of her health a milder climate was recommended & it happened that she was pressed to submit to this trial one day while in a state of [threatening *del.*] alarming debility she was inhaling the fresh air within a tent placed upon a knoll by the side of Conistone Waters, & in view of one of the loveliest of those scenes which we have passed thro' [a climate which *del.*] she was pressed to submit to this [*?* trial] fixing her glistening eyes [were fixed *del.*] upon the beautiful landscape, with an earnestness & even an impatience of voice & manner almost unnatural to her character she answered that if she could not be well with such a heavenly sight before her [eyes *del.*] she could be well no where.

*18. 355–390 By this appropriation ... imagined.] *Our transcription is not always certain, for the deletions, insertions, and rewritings are not clearly distinguishable, and phrases are often barely legible. Underneath the deletions and insertions the first version can be read with some certainty*: By this enclosure [has been *del.*] recently made, agriculture has gained little [by it *del.*] & liberty & taste have lost much. In the wall that bounds this obnoxious enclosure is yet to be seen the [fr *del.*] [remnant *del.*] of a decaying yew tree in within [*sic*] which some contemplative [person *del.*] Man had formerly erected a seat capable of holding only one person from which the solitary humour of the framer may not unfairly be inferred. Here a wayworn traveller might have found a grateful resting-place for standing by the road side it held out a [?]tious invitation [junipers *del.*] and protected from the wind [*& del.*] or the sun for the boughs had been trained to bend round the seat and almost embrace the Person sitting within allowing only an opening for the beautiful Landscape. The narrow space between the [seat *del.*] Yew tree *&* the Lake was scattered over with juniper furze heath *&* wild time.

*20. 391 *After* large *part of a* MS. *deletion reads*: [? grand *del.*] round peninsulas these [?] are attached to the shore one of these called Strickland ears as if the shape *&* the manner in which it is attached to the shore [?] to have reminded someone's fancy of human ears One of these called Strickland ears probably [for *del.*] instead of Stricklands ear the s being [? transferred] to the end of the word [? because] it passes more easily off the tongue.

**20. 400–440 MS. *A is so heavy with deletions and rewritings of identical phrases and sentences that we will record only those variants which differ markedly from the revised version in* MS. Prose 23^{e}. ¶ 400–401 the ground ... removed MS.: for the sides of none of those lakes [? have as *del.*] were graced with houses more suitable in shape *&* size to their situations or more happily distributed — standing removed MS. *A*.

***20. 401 *After* dwellings MS. *deletes*: a [foreigner *del.*] house whose [size *del.*] [? stature *del.*] figure *&* appearance proclaim it to be of foreign extraction has indeed lately sprung among them. [one may be permitted to regret this intrusion as the habitation which it supplanted *del.*] it has not only supplanted an ancient habitation of most becoming appearance but has destroyed [interfered with a <?> the <?> *del.*] injuring [*altered from* injured] the characteristic beauty of the whole scene.

****20. 407–410 fabrics ... ground MS.: fabrics [? had require *del.*] for their size require the enlargement all over which they cannot always obtain the destruction of boundaries that did not press too closely upon their humble [*or* ? humbler] predecessors MS. *A*.

*21. 422–426 its surface ... Lomond] *Some versions of* MS. *A read*: its surface and the network which [faint *del.*] light airs and breath of wind weave upon its restless bos: the points of light which sparkle: diamonds which sparkle in the sun[? shine]: frame of its liquid materials along its surface [is as fine as that which *del.*] equals in fineness that which is woven for the ample surface of

Windermere: The myriads of its and [its diamonds *del.*] & its sparkling points of light [?]ts unnumbered [?] as bright as those the sun on [? waterfall *del.*].

*23. 475 *In* MSS. Verse 57 *Wordsworth began a description of a tour from Ambleside to Keswick. Because he quickly abandoned it, we regard the fragment as the equivalent of a deletion, and merely record it here, as appropriately following the approach to Windermere and preceding the description of Borrowdale; the first two paragraphs below are in Mary Wordsworth's hand*:

From Ambleside to Keswick [enquires *del.*] [says *del.*] (explains the bustling leader of a party of Tourists, glancing his eye carelessly on the map in his hand or casting a look towards the clouds for information concerning the state of the weather) is how far? 16 miles. Is there any thing worthy of notice on the road? Nothing but what all Travellers see as they pass along — will probably be the answer of mine host of the Salutation if the question be asked at the height of the season & he is anxious to have his horses back again for a fresh job & the Post boy will confirm the [observation *del.*] asseveration if necessary for it being a point of feeling with him to hate all stoppages for which he does not receive extra pay. Humanity for his horses also will interfere if his [judg *del.*] mind be unbiassed by selfish expectation & the[ir *del.*] patient & solid claims to consideration of his old companions will be more regarded than the curiosity of a Stranger which he deems odd and fantastic.

But are there not some celebrated Waterfalls not far from the road? Oh yes, Sir, I had forgotten them replies the [the *Edd.*: to MS.] veracious informant apparently [anxious *del.*] thankful to be set right you must al-light [*sic*] in the Village of Rydal & they may be seen in 1/2 an hour. That ½ hour is given to the purpose for usage & fashion require it & for the rest of the journey the Party are contented with what they can collect [? for the *del.*] by their eyes some from the barouche box others from their seat in the open Landau with occasional upstandings upon especial summons or with the presentations through the windows of a close Chariot as the several vehicles are [driven *del.*] whirled along at the rate of 7 miles an hour.

Wordsworth's hand writes an earlier version of the end of the fragment: and for the rest of the journey the party [proceed *del.*] are contented with what they can collect with their eyes from the barouch box, [and *del.*] others [with occa *del.*] from the seat of the open Landau, with occasional upstandings upon especial invitation or with such [appearances *del.*] as [?] presentations of through the loopholes of a close Chariot as the several vehicles whirl along at the rate of 7 miles an hour — But if the Author is to proceed at this rate what must become of the Book which he has undertaken to write — or [if you will *del.*] — to make — No — shall he [?] the next act [?] he has his staff in his hand — the satchel by his side, [as <?> *del.*] or his knapsack at his back [*the rest is illegible*].

*33. 167–186 making us ... Pikes MS. Prose 28[a]: MS. Prose 28[b] *deletes*: making us conscious of its presence. This is so strikingly true with respect to the forms of Nature that the qualities of beauty will almost be entirely overlooked by a Spectator in an object where they may exist [are *undel.* MS.[2]] [involved MS.[2]] in a sublime object with which he may be unfamiliar. [As I do not <mean *del.*> wish to weary the Reader with dry & abstract *undel.*] speculations I will at once refer to the [a MS.[2]] mountainous Country, as into such we are about to enter, in illustration of my notions of the sublime as it exists in landscape. [Let us *undel.*] fix [turn MS.[2]] our eyes together upon [towards MS.[2]] that cluster of mountains at the head of Windermere they [it MS.[2]] is probable that they will settle ere [long upon the Pikes *undel.*]

*35. 218 *After* power MS. *deletes*: as produced by lines [? for] the production of pleasure & pain, good or evil change for the overcoming of resistance and the production of change for fear, for pleasure and pain, for good and for evil. These feelings are conveyed.

*35. 224 *After* precipitous *a caret and an X would seem to indicate a place for an insertion, but we can find nothing marked for insertion.* to compleat MS.[2]: lastly MS. *After* power MS. *deletes*: is imparted to the mind [by mountains from <? the> torrents *del.*] [by <? that> *del.*] by the individual Mountain or a cluster of Mountains [from the *del.*] at the head of Langdale which we have been contemplating, by.

*36. 234 *After at least two false starts at a new paragraph, the* MS. *draws a broad line below the paragraph ending at* 234; *above this line and immediately after* the sun, &c., *the phrase* Thus has been *is inserted. This insertion makes it clear that everything below the line, whether deleted or not, is to be regarded as a deletion, for the revised text begins again on the next page of the MS. with the same phrase,* Thus has been. *The first part of the deleted matter has so many marks of deletion and insertion that the chronology and continuity of the variants cannot be positively asserted, but the deleted and undeleted sentences seem to have been developed in the following way:*

And the power of these outlines convey the feelings of danger & sudden change or by dim analogies to active [power *del.*] force as expressed by the [? to] parts of the human body such as shoulders or head or neck [exceeding heigh *del.*] is invigorated when the outlines by which these perturbed & violent sensations are [included *del.*] [intimated by individual form *del.*] are contrasted with the serenity, the depth & evanescence of form in MS.

These outlines also affect us not merely by sensations referable to motion but by dim analogies which they bear to such parts of organized bodies as height of stature head neck shoulders back breast &c. [as the seats and instruments of active force *del.*] which are dignified in our estimation as being the seats & instruments of active force MS.[2].

The influence of these lines is heightened if the mountain before us be not overtopped by or included in others [it *del.*] but does itself [form the ho *del.*] form a boundary of the horizon for thus all these turbulent or awful sensations of power are excited in immediate contrast with the fathomless depth & the serenity of the sky or in contrast of another [*altered from* other] kind the permanent mountain's individual form is opposed to the fleeting or changeful [change *del.*] clouds which pass over it or lastly the sense of grandeur which it excites is heightened by the powers of the atmosphere [with *del.*] that are visibly allied with it MS.[3].

*44. 465–67 cannot ... intercourse MS.[3]: do nevertheless demand a [previous exercise & discipline & *del.*] certain degree of exercise discipline & familiarity if not with the individual object at least with the [class *del.*] species of objects to which it belongs unlike a [? cer] [?] cannot [make this *del.*] be imparted by an object MS.: cannot [be *del.*] easily be perceived without a process of learning to see and to feel & a certain degree of intercourse MS.[2].

APPENDIX

Hawkshead & the Ferry

12–18. Tall fir ... road] For other descriptions of clipped trees in the neighbourhood of Coniston and Esthwaite, see *C.N.B.* i.511 and 1228. Topiary works became widely popular in the Tudor and Jacobean eras; Evelyn Cecil quotes a gardening manual of 1618 by William Lawson: "Your Gardiner can frame your lesser wood to the shape of men armed in the field, ready to give battell: or swift-running Grey Hounds to chase the Deere, or hunt the Hare. This kind of hunting shall not waste your corne, nor much your coyne." See *A History of Gardening in England*, 3rd edn. (1910) 106. Addison in 1712 (*The Spectator*, № 414) and Pope in 1713 (*The Guardian*, № 173) were among the first to object to ornamental gardening (ibid., 227–8).

64–70. I have ... stared at] Wordsworth refers to the "Introduction" of *S.V.*, or *Guide*, 1688–917. The phrase "flaring edifices" in 66 recalls his quotation from Gray's journal in *Guide*, 1710–13; the comment on "that craving for extensive prospect" which leads to the building of houses that "stare" and are "stared at" verbally echoes *Guide*, 1825–30.

82–99. In the first ... adorn it] The Baptist Chapel dates from 1678; it is thought that the building was originally an ancient cottage. The income-producing land was Sawrey Ground, a farm with which the Chapel was endowed in 1707; in the burying-ground, which was still being used at the beginning of this century, the earliest stone is dated 1750. Cf. Henry S. Cowper, *Hawkshead* (1899) 21, 122–3; and *Victoria History of ... Lancaster*, viii.380. In a note dated October 1922 and appended to his transcript of Wordsworth's manuscript, Gordon Wordsworth wrote: "The dipping pool ... lies in a garden adjoining the Cemetery — It measures about 6 feet by 3, and is formed of large slate slabs, and provided with steps for ingress — The runner still flows into [it], but a neighbour informs me it has now quite fallen out of use."

112–116. gill ... ghyll] Gordon Wordsworth in his transcript of this passage notes that *gill* is Mary Wordsworth's spelling, *& ghyll* Wordsworth's.

125–27. Ezek. 37:3.

128–265. As our textual n. to 80–133 indicates, 80–133 was written later and marked for insertion at the end of 80. But no adjustments were made for the insertion, and as a result an awkward repetition occurs in 128–9. ("we are soon after greeted by the white Church of Hawkshead standing conspicuously on a Hill") *&* 146–7 ("On the top of the hill ... stands the Church, overlooking the Valley").

128–129. we are ... salutation] Cf. *Prel.* IV.13–15.

133–140. The fifteenth-century gate-house may possibly be a rebuilding of the earlier manor house built by the monks of Furness; although later reconstructed, the south wing, containing the hall and solar, was also fifteenth-century; this wing was pulled down about 1870 (*Victoria History of ... Lancaster*, viii.377–9).

In 136–140 Wordsworth follows almost verbatim West's *Antiquities* (1774) xxxvi–xxxvii ("There is, at a small distance from Hawkshead, the house wherein the abbot of Furness kept residence," et cetera), except for variants in punctuation and the alteration of "abbots" to "Abbot" (140).

140–150, textual n. The Vestry, of which Wordsworth complains, was added to the Church in 1793–5. Cf. T.W. Thompson, *Hawkshead Church, Chapelry, and Parish*, 2nd edn. (1959) 16–17.

141–43. Passing ... Abbot] "it is always supposed, and probably correctly, that the monastic 'furca' was on Gallow-barrow." Cf. H.S. Cowper, *Hawkshead* (1899) 226.

143–145. we arrive ... hills] The phrasing oddly echoes Clarke (146): "Hawkshead, a little market-town about four miles from Ambleside, pleasantly situated at the foot of a range of small mountains, covered chiefly with wood."

150. Archbishop Sandes] Edwin Sandys (1516–1588) was probably born at Esthwaite Hall, his father's estate; an extreme Protestant, he was imprisoned in the Tower for having supported Lady Jane Grey's claim to the throne in 1553, and was later self-exiled to the Continent until the succession of Elizabeth. He was made Bishop of Worcester in 1559, Bishop of London in 1570, and Archbishop of York in 1575. Royal Letters Patent for the founding of the Grammar School were issued in 1585; Sandys drew up his Statutes for the school three months before his death in 1588. See *Victoria History of ... Lancaster*, viii. 371; H.S. Cowper, *Hawkshead* (1899) 463 ff. Wordsworth paid tribute to the founder of his school in "Lines Written as a School Exercise at Hawkshead" (*P.W.* i.260): "Then noble Sandys, inspir'd with great design, / Reared Hawkshead's happy roof, and call'd it mine."

157–185. A fisherman ... comynwealth] Clarke (147) touches briefly on the Pilgrimage of Grace in 1536 and then goes on to say that the people of Hawkshead "chose for their General one Robert Aske, a man of low parentage, and one Rudston for his assistant: others they had of the same stamp; as a fisherman from this town, who stiled himself (and very justly) the *Earl of Poverty*; he always went by that name, and signed himself so." Clarke (148) quotes the unsigned announcement, or "Summons," which Wordsworth copies with only minor differences (the parenthesis in 1278 is an interpolation of Wordsworth's). According to Clarke, the "pilgrims" got as far as Doncaster where they were met by the Duke of Norfolk, who agreed to carry their demands to the king; Henry refused the demands, but granted a general pardon and the 'pilgrims' dispersed. Clarke (151) then concludes: "the year following, Robert Ask the General, Lord Dacres, the Abbot and Prior of Saurey near Hawkshead, *&c.* rising again, were taken *&* beheaded. I have inserted this for nothing more than to shew what illiterate warlike people this northern part of England was inhabited by." For a briefer account, see *Victoria History of … Lancaster,* viii.299.

194, textual n. Caprice … skill] This fragmentary sentence, which is deleted from the bottom of page [2^r] and the top of page [2^v], MS. Prose 23^b, apparently derives from some other context, unknown to us.

195–201. Along the … beneath] Cf. *Prel.* V. 423–31. The stone seat is today unchanged.

206–11. Upon a … mystery] Cf. Gilpin, i. 96: "how deep & determined the shadows are at noon." For martial figures seen in the clouds, cf. *Prel.* II, textual n. 181–3 (3), & p. 522; "To the Clouds," II. 11–14 (*P.W.* ii.317).

216–254. The table tomb to the memory of William Sandys and his wife Margaret is described in *Victoria History of … Lancaster,* viii. 372–3, which also quotes the Latin inscription.

In his memoir of Elizabeth Smith (1776–1806), De Quincey, who did not know the Smiths until after Elizabeth's death, deplored the simplicity of the marble tablet to her memory: "After mentioning her birth and age (twenty-nine), it closes thus: — "She possessed great talents, exalted virtues, and humble piety." Anything so unsatisfactory or so commonplace I have rarely known." See *Collected Writings,* ed. D. Masson (*Commentary*: Unpublished Tour 1889) ii.418; De Quincey's essay was first published in *Tail's Magazine* (June 1840). Wordsworth, who also did not know Elizabeth Smith, probably acquired his information from his friend Thomas Wilkinson, who was a close friend of the Smiths and a great admirer of Elizabeth's. If Wordsworth had read the memoirs to which he refers, he would have found that Elizabeth's unusual linguistic attainments (French, German, Hebrew, Arabic, Persian) were well known in her lifetime. The 'memoirs,' compiled by Henrietta Maria Bowdler, are entitled *Fragments, in Prose and Verse: By a Young Lady, Lately Deceased. With Some Account of her Life and Character, by The Author of "Sermons on the Doctrines and Duties of Christianity"* (1808); a second edition in two volumes was published in Bath, 1809. The Smiths, whose home was originally at Piercefield Park in Monmouthshire, moved to Patterdale in 1800 and to Coniston in 1801; at Coniston, Elizabeth sometimes walked twelve to fourteen hours a day (*Fragments,* 179) and Thomas Wilkinson in his letter and verses published by Mrs. Bowdler in the *Fragments* (203–9) makes much of her mountain climbing. From a letter written by her mother soon after her death, and also published in the *Fragments,* we learn that in her last invalid year Elizabeth rested on warm days in a tent pitched near the house and that there she once responded to a proposal that she spend the winter months in Cornwall with the words, "If I cannot live here, I am sure I can no where else" (*Fragments,* 190). As late as the I.F. note to "To the Spade of a Friend" (*P.W.* iv.416), Wordsworth recalls Thomas Wilkinson's having been honoured by the friendship of Elizabeth Smith.

265–66, textual n. Gordon Wordsworth's insertion here of the first paragraph given in our textual n. 140–150 not only seems to lack the authority of any manuscript direction, but also would seem to come much too late in the description, since the point of view in textual n. 140–150 is that of a traveller approaching the village from Hawkshead Hall, a little to the north of Hawkshead.

278–85. a floating grove ... diminishes] Cf. *Guide,* 966–74 and n. The "island," which has now disappeared, was described by John Housman, *A Descriptive Tour, and Guide to the Lakes, Caves, Mountains, and Other Natural Curiosities, in Cumberland, Westmoreland, Lancashire* (1800) 180, and mentioned by John Britton, *The Beauties of England and Wales* (1807) ix.95.

286–305. Adjoining ... stood] That an "Ecclesiastic" had drowned in the pool at the head of Esthwaite Water seems to have been a tradition not founded on fact; from the name *Priest Pot,* Henry S. infers that the pool had once been "a private fishery pertaining to Hawkshead Hall." See Cowper, *Hawkshead* (1899) 43.

In 1672 Thomas Lancaster was hanged for having poisoned his wife and several members of her family. "The place where the gibbet stood at Pool Stang is yet called Gibbet Moss, and lies just beyond the pool bridge going to Colthouse on the right hand of the road. Although we are unaware of any record of any other hanging taking place here, and although it would appear from the entry [in the Parish Register Book] that a special gibbet was placed here for Lancaster, it is a fact that elderly people can still remember the stump of the gibbet standing; nay more, superstitions had grown up connected with it" (Cowper, 226); although no apparition was connected with Gibbet Moss, the place was thought to be haunted *&* "so long as the stumps of the grim gibbet were standing ... people dreaded it even by daylight" (ibid., 326).

Wordsworth's description of Gibbet Moss will for most readers evoke one of the most famous "spots of time" recorded in *The Prelude* (XI.279–316). The scenery around Hawkshead in the late eighteenth century could well accord with that given in *The Prelude*, especially if one of the near-by eminences had then had a beacon on its summit; although we know of no beacon near Hawkshead, we recall a possibly relevant statement in West's *Antiquities*: "Furness is surrounded with beacons, which might receive the alarm from those at a distance in any quarter; but whether they be ancient or modern cannot be determined" (1774) xi, and (1806) 11. We also recall that in neighbouring Westmorland beacons were numerous everywhere: "There has scarcely been five miles without a beacon. ... Many of them still retain the name of beacons as indicative of their original designation." See *Lonsdale Magazine*, iii (1822) 250. The descriptions of the area around Penrith Beacon as given by Hutchinson (*Excursion*, 52–3), Gilpin (ii.85), and Clarke (22) would seem to make Cowdrake Quarry, near Penrith Beacon, which Gordon Wordsworth identified as the setting for the episode in *The Prelude* (*Prel.*, 614) less likely than the neighbourhood of Gibbet Moss. Nevertheless Wordsworth himself plainly connected the event in *The Prelude* with Penrith Beacon (cf. *Prel.* VI.239–45 and XI.317–23), and accordingly we are inclined to believe that later experiences at Hawkshead modified his recollection of a gibbet seen near Penrith when he was "not six years old" (*Prel.* VI.280). One sign, in particular, of a modification is that in MS.V, *Prel.* XI.290, Wordsworth wrote that the man who was hanged was "the murderer of his wife" and this statement is true of Thomas Lancaster at Hawkshead, but not true of the murderer near Penrith (*Prel.*, 614).

293. in the solitudes of Salisbury Plain] Cf. the Sailor's experience on Salisbury Plain in *Guilt and Sorrow*, 76–81 (*P.W.* i.98)

> Now, as he plodded on, with sullen clang
> A sound of chains along the desert rang;
> He looked, and saw upon a gibbet high
> A human body that in irons swang,
> Uplifted by the tempest whirling by;
> And, hovering, round it often did a raven fly.

299–300. the Bittern ... 1740] From the statement here we assume that line 25 in *An Evening Walk* (1793) has a literary, rather than a factual, origin: "when first the vales the bittern fills" (*P.W.* i.6).

323–353. Cf. our n. to *Guide*, 907–18. The history of the two pairs of swans on Esthwaite & of those brought by John Christian Curwen to Windermere is repeated in the I.F. note to *An Evening Walk* (*P.W.* i.319).

354–371. Cf. "Lines left upon a Seat in a Yew-tree" (*P.W.* i.92–4). In *U.T.* Wordsworth repeats details which he had given in the poem and adds others which he was to repeat in the I.F. note to the poem (*P.W.* i.329). For example, in the poem the "aged Tree" had been "taught ... With its dark arms to form a circling bower" (cf. 361–365), & from this seat the recluse would look out on "barren rocks, with fern & heath, / And juniper and thistle, sprinkled o'er" (cf. 366–67). The effects of the "obnoxious enclosure" (1471), a "slip of poor cultivated land" (354–55), are at the beginning of the I.F. note similarly deplored: "the slip of Common on which it [the yew-tree] stood, that ran parallel to the lake, and lay open to it, has long been enclosed; so that the road has lost much of its attraction" (cf. 354–59). The man of "solitary humour" (*U.T.*, textual n. 355–391) is, in the I.F. note, identified as "a gentleman of the neighbourhood ... who had been educated at one of our Universities, and returned to pass his time in seclusion on his own estate. He died a bachelor in middle age." In addition to the seat in the yew-tree on Esthwaite's north-eastern shore, he was induced "by the beauty of the prospect" to build "a small summer-house on the rocks above the peninsula on which the [Windermere] ferry-house stands" (I.F. note).

The builder of the yew-tree seat has been identified as the Revd. William Braithwaite of Satterhow, Far Sawrey, who according to the Hawkshead Parish Register died at Hawkshead, 8 February 1800, aged forty-six. See Moorman, i.312; W.J.B. Owen, ed., *Lyrical Ballads* (1967) 127–8; Mark L. Reed, *Wordsworth: The Chronology of the Early Years* (1967) 291. The identification, based on the fact that Braithwaite built the 'Pleasure-house' above the ferry (cf. *S.V.* 96–114 and n.), seems somewhat surprising, if not improbable: in the poem, published in 1798, the recluse is said to have died "In this deep vale ... this seat his only monument" (*P.W.* i.93); before his death, Braithwaite had acquired the piece of land on the shore of Esthwaite (Moorman, i.312) whose alteration would have offended the "contemplative Man" of *U.T.* On the other hand, we have not been able to discover any evidence that "a small summer-house" had once stood on the site where in the late nineties Braithwaite built his house, although a remark in the I.F. note (*P.W.* i.329) about a time "some years before the first pleasure-house was built" might imply such a building.

Of the yew-tree, Henry S. Cowper writes: "although the real tree was destroyed by Mr. Braithwaite Hodgson, of Green End, in Wordsworth's lifetime, another stands not far from the site, and has been called by the name of, and we believe is pointed out as, 'Wordsworth's Yew.'" See *Hawkshead* (1899) 416–17.

357–59. it has ... lake] In the I.F. note referred to in our preceding n., Wordsworth, after remarking that the road "has lost much of its attraction," adds that "This spot was my favourite walk in the evenings during the latter part of my school-time." Mark L. Reed (op. cit., 291) misreads the I.F. note and says that it was to this spot that the boy Wordsworth led a child of his own age for the sake of witnessing the child's pleasure upon first seeing the view; this episode, which Wordsworth recalls in the I.F. note (*P.W.* i.329), occurred not near the yew-tree seat, but on the 'Station' overlooking the more spectacular view of Windermere and its islands.

376–79. We have ... distance] i.e., 1377–80 above.

391–94. But it ... Strickland-ears] Cf. *Prel.* V.456–8: "I chanced to cross / One of those open fields, which, shaped like ears, / Make green peninsulas on Esthwaite's Lake."

398–99. the Stranger ... quoted] Apparently it had been Wordsworth's intention to quote the praise of some "Stranger" to Hawkshead parish.

440. black & steep as a wall] Cf. *An Evening Walk* (1793) I.372 (*P.W.* i.34): "Like a black wall, the mountain steeps appear."

440–43. Above ... the lake] Cf. textual n. 98.

455–54. Cf. *An Evening Walk* (1793) II.339–50 (*P.W.* i.32):

> —"Mid the dark steeps repose the shadowy streams,
> As touch'd with dawning moonlight's hoary gleams,
> Long streaks of fairy light the wave illume
> With bordering lines of intervening gloom,
> Soft o'er the surface creep the lustres pale
> Tracking with silvering path the changeful gale.
> —'Tis restless magic all; at once the bright
> Breaks on the shade, the shade upon the light,
> Fair Spirits are abroad; in sportive chase
> Brushing with lucid wands the water's face,
> While music stealing round the glimmering deeps
> Charms the tall circle of th' enchanted steeps.

The variants in our text are not recorded in the textual apparatus of *P.W.* i.32–3, nor are they preserved in the final text of 1849, II.291–304, *P.W.* i.33.

447. The word *faint* is inserted without any further alteration to the line.

COMMENTARY II

The Sublime & the Beautiful

131–186. amongst them ... Pikes] It is, we think, impossible to estimate the amount of text lost from the beginning of MSS. Prose 28. In our description of the manuscripts (see 148–9), we have suggested that page [2^{r}] of MS. Prose 28^{b} was originally the first page of that particular leaflet; in any case, pages [1^{r}] & [1^{v}] of MS. Prose 28^{b} are blank & the text of this leaflet begins, on page [2^{r}], with the rejected passage which is recorded in textual n. 39–58. The revised and amplified version which was substituted for this rejected passage begins seven lines from the bottom of page [1^{v}] and ends 3 in. from the bottom of page [2^{r}] in MS. Prose 28^{a}. Since the extant text of MS. Prose 28^{a} (*Subl. and Beaut.*, 1–58) is entirely coherent, we suppose that just as 39–58 ("making us ... Pikes") is substituted for the rejected passage in MS. Prose 28^{b}, so 1–38 ("amongst them ... precedes the beautiful in") must be a substitution for a rejected passage immediately preceding the one that still survives. In other words, we believe that MS. Prose 28^{a} is a revised draft, written for insertion in MS. Prose 28^{b}.

The question then of what has been lost from the opening turns out to be a double-barrelled one: first, what preceded the deletion now preserved in textual n. 39–58, and secondly, what preceded the phrase "amongst them" in the opening of the revised extant text? If the recurrent "3" in the manuscript page-numbering (see Owen & Smyser's description of the manuscripts, 148–9) indicates either a third leaflet or a third section, then the loss may have been fairly extensive; but from the statements made in 168–70 & 180–83, it would seem that the loss from the discussion of the sublime and the beautiful has, at least, been minimal.

131–137. It is … knowledge] Wordsworth is rejecting eighteenth-century views stemming from Addison's theory that the "*new* or *uncommon*" is a characteristic of objects pleasurable to the imagination (*The Spectator*, ed. D.F. Bond (1965) № 412, iii. 540–2); for example, John Baillie had maintained that "Admiration, a Passion always attending the Sublime, arises from *Uncommonness*, and constantly decays as the Object becomes more and more familiar." See "An Essay on the Sublime" (1747), *The Augustan Reprint Society*, № 43 (1953) 12. In insisting that "astonishment … is the effect of the sublime in its highest degree," Burke implied a similar view. See *A Philosophical Enquiry into the Origin of our Ideas of the Sublime and Beautiful*, ed. J.T. Boulton (1958) 57.

143. love … the one] Cf. Burke, *Enquiry*, 91: "By beauty I mean, that quality or those qualities in bodies by which they cause love, or some passion similar to it."

151. the same object … beautiful] Cf. Wordsworth's letter to Jacob Fletcher quoted in our n. to 257–78. Whereas Addison (*The Spectator*, № [452] 412, iii. 541, 544) recognized the superiority of those objects in which the sublime and the beautiful are united, Burke implied that because of their antithetical differences, the two qualities almost never occur in the same object (e.g., *Enquiry* 5, 124–5, 156–7, 160); in his second edition, he commented upon the occasional exception: "In the infinite variety of natural combinations we must expect to find the qualities of things the most remote imaginable from each other united in the same object. … If the qualities of the sublime and beautiful are sometimes found united, does this prove, that they are the same, does it prove, that they are any way allied, does it prove even that they are not opposite and contradictory? Black and white may soften, may blend, but they are not therefore the same. Nor when they are so softened and blended with each other, or with different colours, is the power of black as black, or of white as white, so strong as when each stands uniform and distinguished" (*Enquiry*, 124–5). On finding beauty and sublimity united at Ullswater, Gilpin (ii. 53–4) sharply protested against Burke's general position. Despite his statement above, Wordsworth in

the *Guide* (e.g., 2543–9, 2739–44) tends to preserve the distinction which Burke habitually stressed.

154–56. the mind ... other] Cf. Burke, *Enquiry*, 160: "the sublime and beautiful are built on principles very different, and ... their affections are as different: the great has terror for its basis; which, when it is modified, causes that emotion in the mind, which I have called astonishment; the beautiful is founded on mere positive pleasure, and excites in the soul that feeling, which is called love." In *Prel.* XIII.143–7, Wordsworth attributes to sublime and beautiful forms his own early apprehension of the universe as "divine and true":

To fear and love,
To love as first and chief, for there fear ends,
Be this ascribed; to early intercourse,
In presence of sublime and lovely Forms,
With the adverse principles of pain and joy.

The sense of beauty and the sense of sublimity are "opposite to each other" in yet another respect: "The primary element in the sense of beauty is a distinct perception of parts" (textual n. 156), whereas the sense of sublimity occurs "without a conscious contemplation of parts" (268–69). Wordsworth's recognition of this difference may owe something to Coleridge, who in a note for one of his lectures of 1808 wrote: "What then if ... we should define beauty to be a pleasurable sense of the many (by many I do not mean comparative multitude, but only as a generic word opposed to absolute unity) reduced to unity by the correspondence of all the component parts to each other, and the reference of all to one central point. ... Now if we receive this definition, we shall at once understand why in correct language beauty has been appropriated to the objects of the eye and ear, for these senses are the only ones that present a whole to us combined with a consciousness of its parts." See S.C., ed. T.M. Raysor (1960) i.162–3. In the *Guide* (871–5) Wordsworth adds an interesting modification to the antithesis between beauty and sublimity: "Sublimity is the result of Nature's first great dealings with the superficies of the earth; but the general tendency of her subsequent operations is towards the production of beauty, by a multiplicity of symmetrical parts uniting in a consistent whole."

161. the present work] See Owen & Smyser's "Introduction to the *Guide*," 131–2.

162–68. Sensations ... its presence] Cf. *Prel.* XIII. 214–32, where Wordsworth recognizes the precedence which sublimity took over beauty in impressing his own youthful mind.

180–83. These shall ... landscape] The work of Wordsworth's predecessors who wrote on the sublime and beautiful in the landscape of the Lake District has been described and evaluated by Christopher Hussey [and others]. See Christopher Hussey, *The Picturesque* (1927), W. M. Merchant, "Introduction" to Wordsworth's *Guide Through the District of the Lakes* (1951), and Norman Nicholson, *The Lakers* (1955).

196–97. a sense of ... power] Cf. *S.V.* 632–7; *U.T.* 981–4; *Guide*, 871–2, 2251–2. Neither individual form nor duration figures in discussions of the sublime in natural scenery before Wordsworth, perhaps because the ocean, which is often cited as the ultimate in sublimity, would preclude individuality of form, while storms and similar 'sublime' disturbances would preclude duration. Burke does, however, mention "momentary duration" in connection with beauty ("the flowery species, so remarkable for its weakness and momentary duration ... gives us the liveliest idea of beauty, & elegance" (*Enquiry*, 116)), and throughout his work he emphasizes power as an element of the sublime: "I know of nothing sublime which is not some modification of power" (64).

197. a sense of power] W.J.B. Owen in *Wordsworth as Critic* (1969) 195–215, has made an interpretative & critical study of Wordsworth's concept of 'power' as a major element in the 'sublime'; see especially 203–10, where important passages of MSS. Prose 28 (i.e., 57–69, 89–102, 140–60, 220–40, 248–55) are quoted and analyzed.

191–234. But ... the sun, *&c.*] Cf. *Prel*, VII.716–29.

218–219. impressions ... elevated] Cf. Burke, *Enquiry*, 50–1: "Now whatever either on good or upon bad grounds tends to raise a man in his own opinion, produces a sort of swelling and triumph that is extremely grateful to the human mind; and this swelling is never more perceived, nor operates with more force, than when without danger we are conversant with terrible objects, the mind always claiming to itself some part of the dignity and importance of the things which it contemplates."

223–25. These lines ... sea] Gilpin (i.88–90) discusses the same mountain lines in relation to picturesque beauty. Cf. *Guide*, 664 and n.

224. danger *&* sudden change] Cf. Burke, *Enquiry*, 39: "Whatever is fitted in any sort to excite the ideas of pain, and danger, that is to say, whatever is in any sort terrible, or is conversant about terrible objects, or operates in a manner analogous to terror, is a source of the sublime"; cf. also ibid., 51, 57–8.

225–28. they may ... not less sublime] Cf. *Guide*, 2184–91 and n.; Burke, *Enquiry*: "hardly any thing can strike the mind with its greatness, which does not make some sort of approach to infinity" (63); and: "Another source of the sublime, is *infinity*. ... Infinity has a tendency to fill the mind with that sort of delightful horror, which is the most genuine effect, and truest test of the sublime ... the eye not being able to perceive the bounds of many things, they seem to be infinite, and they produce the same effects as if they were really so" (ibid., 73).

231. its] The faulty pronominal reference is the result of abortive rewritings; from textual nn. 230, 232–33, it would seem that Wordsworth originally had intended to write: "this sense of power is imparted to the mind by the individual Mountain or a cluster of Mountains ... by the torrents ... by the clouds ... by the stature ...," *&c.*

232–33. the stature … sky] *Paradise Lost,* IV. 988 ("His stature reacht the Skie"), quoted and praised in *P. 1815,* 361–6. James Scoggins observes that in 1803 Dorothy Wordsworth had used the same phrase to characterize sublime mountain forms (*Journals,* i.332). See Scoggins, *Imagination & Fancy* (1966) 162.

234, textual n. these outlines also affect us … active force] Cf. *Prel.* I. 406–12 ("a huge Cliff, / As if with voluntary power instinct, / Uprear'd its head… / And, growing still in stature… / Strode after me"); *Prel.* XIII. 45 ("A hundred hills their dusky backs upheaved").

251–53. an individual cloud … body] Although it is not included among Blake's songs copied into Wordsworth's Commonplace Book, dated "Grasmere Jan^{RY} 1800" (Wordsworth Library, MS. Prose 31), Wordsworth may be remembering, among other "tales & pictures," the introductory poem to *Songs of Innocence*: "On a cloud I saw a child, / And he laughing said to me."

264–65. starting trees] In his description of Gordale Scar, quoted in our n. to *Guide,* 45, Gray similarly used the word *starting*: "with stubbed yew-trees and shrubs starting from its sides." Cf. *O.E.D.,* s.v. *start,* 3.d ("Of a plant: To spring up suddenly. *rare*").

265–66. if personal fear … bounds] The observation is commonplace in discussions of the sublime: e.g., Addison, *The Spectator,* № 418, iii.568, and Burke, *Enquiry,* 136; W.J.B. Owen cites in this connection Richard Payne Knight, *An Analytical Inquiry into the Principles of Taste,* 2nd edn. (1805) 55–6. See Owen, *Wordsworth as Critic,* n. 29, 204.

266–70. For whatever … sublime] Cf. 153–56 and n.; *S.V.* 245–8; *Guide,* 2188–90: "For sublimity will never be wanting, where the sense of innumerable multitude is lost in, and alternates with, that of intense unity"; Burke, *Enquiry,* 57: "The passion caused by the great and sublime in *nature* … is Astonishment; and astonishment is that state of the soul, in which all its motions are suspended, with some degree of horror.

In this case the mind is so entirely filled with its object, that it cannot entertain any other, nor by consequence reason on that object which employs it"; Alexander Gerard, *Essay on Taste* (1759) 19: "Objects exciting terror are ... in general sublime; for terror always implies astonishment, occupies the whole soul, and suspends all its motions."

276–79. Power ... upon it] Cf. Addison, *The Spectator*, № 412, iii.540: "Our Imagination loves to be filled with an Object, or to graspe at any thing that is too big for its Capacity"; Gerard, *Essay on Taste*, 14: "We always contemplate objects and ideas with a disposition similar to their nature. When a large object is presented, the mind expands itself to the extent of that object, and is filled with one grand sensation, which totally possessing it, composes it into a solemn sedateness, and strikes it with deep silent wonder and admiration: it finds such a difficulty in spreading itself to the dimensions of its object, as enlivens and invigorates its frame: and having overcome the opposition which this occasions, it sometimes imagines itself present in every part of the scene, which it contemplates."

285. the head & the front] *Othello*, I.iii.80; cf. *Cintra*, 2609–10.

289. takes place of] "takes precedence over"; cf. *Cintra*, 2889; *R.M.* 444–5; *Guide*, 1976.

301–05. Belial ... Eternity?] *Paradise Lost*, II.146–8: "for who would lose, / Though full of pain, this intellectual being, / Those thoughts that wander through eternity ... ?"

310–13. how industrious ... despite] Cf. *E.E.* III.11–12: "Now, vice and folly are in contradiction with the moral principle which can never be extinguished in the mind"; the sentence following contains a reference to Milton's Satan.

318–19. As I ... before] i.e., 266–68.

324–25. our moral Nature ... violated] Cf. "Prospectus," 19–22, to *The Excursion*, quoted in our n. to 280–2.

325–27. The point ... carried] Wordsworth should have written: "The point to which apprehensions ... may be carried," or "The point beyond which apprehensions ... may not be carried." Cf. these two passages: "if personal fear be strained beyond a certain point, this sensation [of the sublime] is destroyed" (270–71); and: "To what degree consistent with sublimity power may be dreaded has been ascertained" (347–49).

330–34. But if ... law] The thought seems essentially stoical: reason, which is the ruling principle in man, discovers what things are within our power & what are not; it directs our exertions towards that which is within our power; obedience to reason preserves inviolate our moral nature (198–9) and culminates in repose. Cf. "Ode to Duty" (*P.W.* iv. 83–6); *Exc.* III.359–406; *R.M.* 422–40; on Wordsworth's stoicism, both ancient and modern, see Jane Worthington, *Wordsworth's Reading of Roman Prose* (1946) 60–9, and N.P. Stallknecht, *Strange Seas of Thought*, 2nd edn. (1958) 204–22, 276–81.

352. as has been determined] i.e., 266–68.

361–72. If the ... vivid] In 1790 Wordsworth wrote to Dorothy of the fall of the Rhine at Schaffhausen, which he had just seen for the first time: "Magnificent as this fall certainly is I must confess I was disappointed in it. I had raised my ideas too high" (*E.Y.*, 35). In the passage in our text, written some twenty years later and long before he had seen the fall for the second time, he illustrates an observation which Coleridge was to make in 1813: "The sense of sublimity arises, not from the sight of an outward object, but from the reflection upon it; not from the impression, but from the idea. Few have seen a celebrated waterfall without feeling something of disappointment: it is only subsequently, by reflection, that the idea of the waterfall comes full into the mind, and brings with it a train of sublime associations." See *S.C.*, i.224. The "fall of the Rhine," but not the rock, is described in *Ecclesiastical Sonnets*, II.xliii (*P.W.* iii.382–3). Cf. also *Guide*, 2681–4; *Journals*, ii. 88–92; M.W., *Letters*, 63.

372–79. Yet to return ... unity] See W.J.B. Owen, *Wordsworth as Critic*, 208–10; Owen cites, in illustration of Wordsworth's generalization, *Prel.* VI.556–72.

379. infinity, which is a modification of unity] Cf. *Guide*, 2184–91 and n.; Kant, *The Critique of Judgment*, tr. J.C. Meredith (1957): "the sublime is to be found in an object even devoid of form, so far as it immediately involves, or else by its presence provokes, a representation of *limitlessness*, yet with a super-added thought of its totality" (90); Burke quoted above in nn. 97–100, 140–4.

381–95. the main source ... affected] Cf. Wordsworth to Jacob Fletcher, 25 Feb. 1825 (*L.Y.*, 184): "our business is not so much with objects as with the law under which they are contemplated. The confusion incident to these disquisitions has I think arisen principally from not attending to this distinction. We hear people perpetually disputing whether this or that thing be beautiful or not — sublime or otherwise, without being aware that the same object may be both beautiful and sublime, but it cannot be felt to be such at the same moment"; see also *L.Y.*, 194–5. In general, eighteenth-century critics analyzed the effects on the mind rather than the qualities of the objects (W.J. Hipple, Jr., *The Beautiful, The Sublime, & The Picturesque in Eighteenth-Century British Æsthetic Theory* (1957) 81, 84), but later Gilpin, Uvedale Price, and numerous topographical writers fixed their attention upon the external object and its qualities; John R. Nabholtz ("Wordsworth's *Guide to the Lakes & the Picturesque Tradition*," *M.P.* lxi (1964) 288–97) has pointed out how Wordsworth himself in the *Guide* frequently follows the latter course.

387–89. To talk ... absurd] Cf. Kant, *The Critique of Judgment*, 104: "true sublimity must be sought only in the mind of the judging Subject, and not in the Object of nature that occasions this attitude by the estimate formed of it," but according to Kant this statement could not be applied to beauty.

403–06. to power ... eternity] For the extent of the manuscript loss see textual n. 403. The governing "intelligence of law & reason" again suggests a stoical philosophy (cf. our n. to 324–29). On the basis of lines 19–22 of the "Prospectus" to *The Excursion* (*P.W.* v. 3), we believe that the lost antecedent of "her" in 405 may have been "the individual Mind" or a semantic equivalent. (The textual n. to ll. 20–22 of the "Prospectus" implies that the lines we quote may be a late revision.)

> Of the individual Mind that keeps her own
> Inviolate retirement, subject there
> To Conscience only, and the law supreme
> Of that Intelligence which governs all.

With 280–2 cf. also *Exc.* IV. 69–76:

> "Possessions vanish, and opinions change,
> And passions hold a fluctuating seat:
> But, by the storms of circumstance unshaken,
> And subject neither to eclipse nor wane,
> Duty exists; — immutably survive,
> For our support, the measures and the forms,
> Which an abstract intelligence supplies;
> Whose kingdom is, where time and space are not."

409. influences] Although the word is plainly written, Wordsworth probably intended "inferences"; if so, "the *means*" in 407 should perhaps be regarded as the antecedent of "them" in 410.

412–26. I have ... cause] Cf. *Guide*, 2476–80; *Railway*, 148–56.

426–30. Such would ... perceiving] Wordsworth summarizes Sir Joshua Reynolds's recollections of his disappointment upon first seeing the paintings of Raphæl in the Vatican and then of his gradually acquiring from them "a new taste and new perceptions." Wordsworth's source was one of Reynolds's "loose papers" quoted by Edmund Malone in *The Works of Sir Joshua Reynolds ... To Which is Prefixed, An Account of the*

Life and Writings of the Author (1797) i.x–xii. Cf. *Ad. L.B.* 32–5, *P.L.B.* 744–7, and nn.

430–444. I have heard … lifeless] On 21 September 1803 Sir Walter Scott told the Wordsworths this anecdote; in retelling it here, Wordsworth seems, in 314–20, to draw verbally on Dorothy's account: "She used to say that in the new world into which she was come nothing had disappointed her so much as trees and woods; she complained that they were lifeless, silent, &, compared with the grandeur of the ever-changing ocean, even insipid" (*Journals*, i. 402).

447–48. Glencoe] Visited by William & Dorothy, September 1803 (*Journals*, i. 330–6).

451–54. the chaotic … unfinished] Cf. *S.V.* textual n. 52, and our n. to *S.V.*, textual nn. 47 and 52.

458–59, textual n. The word "in" is clear, but it is perhaps an error for "of."

458–463. that intermixture … afflictions] Cf. Coleridge on *Hamlet*: "The terrible, however paradoxical it may appear, will be found to touch on the verge of the ludicrous. Both arise from the perception of something out of the common nature of things. … These complex causes will naturally have produced in Hamlet the disposition to escape from his own feelings of the overwhelming and supernatural by a wild transition to the ludicrous." See *S.C.*, ii. 224–5.

472–74. it is … sublimity] Cf. 165–68 and our n. to 162–68.

477–91. But I … mind] In *Prel.* XI. 148–64, Wordsworth recalls his own brief submission to the false æsthetic theories of the age:

> through presumption, even in pleasure pleas'd
> Unworthily, disliking here, and there,
> Liking, by rules of mimic art transferr'd
> To things above all art.
>
> (XI. 152–5)

According to Gilpin, nature succeeds in harmonizing colors, but "is seldom so correct in composition, as to produce an harmonious whole. Either the foreground, or the background, is disproportioned: or some awkward line runs across the piece: or a tree is ill-placed: or a bank is formal: or something or other is not exactly what it should be." See Gilpin, *Observations on the River Wye*, 2nd edn. (1789) 81; some years later, writing of Windermere, he found fault with both the east and west shores, and although the Langdale Pikes at the head were "grand," he concluded that because of its extensiveness, "This great scene ... surveyed thus from a centre, was rather amusing, than picturesque." See Gilpin, i.153.

488. *picturesque*] Uvedale Price, whose own landscaping exhibited for Wordsworth too "delicate and fastidious" a taste (*M.Y.* i.505–6, but see also *M.Y.* i.3), had made the *picturesque* a category distinct from the sublime and the beautiful. See *An Essay on the Picturesque* (1796) i.46–61, 229–43. For Wordsworth's definition of the word *picturesque*, see *L.Y.*, 173, 183–4.

In 1812 Dorothy Wordsworth wrote of the Revd. C.J. Blomfield: "B's views of everything he sees are contracted by his love of the picturesque — his amiable disposition and his sensibility will I have little doubt in time overcome this — and after a few visits to the North he will find that there is a wider range of enjoyment here than he at present conceives." See *M.Y.* ii.41.

COLOPHON

FRAGMENTS was typeset in InDesign 5.0.

The text, titles, and page numbers are set in *Adobe Jenson Pro.*

Book design & typesetting: Alessandro Segalini

Cover design: Contra Mundum Press

Cover image: Up for Air, Langdale Pikes © 2011 Stewart Smith Photography. Shot date: January 21, 2011

FRAGMENTS

is published by Contra Mundum Press

and printed by Lightning Source, which has received Chain of

Custody certification from: The Forest Stewardship Council,

The Programme for the Endorsement of Forest Certification,

and The Sustainable Forestry Initiative.

CONTRA MUNDUM PRESS

Contra Mundum Press is dedicated to the value & the indispensable importance of the individual voice.

Contra Mundum Press will be publishing titles from all the fields in which the genius of the age traditionally produces the most challenging and innovative work: poetry, novels, theatre, philosophy — including philosophy of science & of mathematics — criticism, and essays. Upcoming volumes include Oğuz Atay's *While Waiting for Fear*, Mallarmé's *The Book*, and Sándor Tar's *Our Street*.

For the complete list of forthcoming publications, please visit our website. To be added to our mailing list, send your name and email address to: info@contramundum.net

Contra Mundum Press
P.O. Box 1326
New York, NY 10276
USA
info@contramundum.net

OTHER CONTRA MUNDUM PRESS TITLES

Gilgamesh
Ghérasim Luca, *Self-Shadowing Prey*
Rainer J. Hanshe, *The Abdication*
Walter Jackson Bate, *Negative Capability*
Miklós Szentkuthy, *Marginalia on Casanova*
Fernando Pessoa, *Philosophical Essays*
Elio Petri, *Writings on Cinema & Life*
Friedrich Nietzsche, *The Greek Music Drama*
Richard Foreman, *Plays with Films*
Louis-Auguste Blanqui, *Eternity by the Stars*
Miklós Szentkuthy, *Towards the One & Only Metaphor*
Josef Winkler, *When the Time Comes*

SOME FORTHCOMING TITLES

Josef Winkler, *Natura Morta*
Fernando Pessoa, *The Transformation Book*
Miklós Szentkuthy, *Prae*
Federico Fellini, *Making a Film*

ACKNOWLEDGEMENTS

I would like to thank Jeff Cowton & Rebecca Turner, the Curator and Assistant Curator, of the Jerwood Centre for their kindness and help in negotiating the manuscripts. They made my labor a pleasure. And I would also like to thank the Wordsworth Trust for allowing us to reproduce a page of this fragile manuscript.

Alan VARDY

Kind regards are due to Lynette Owen for her congeniality and patience, though it is most especially her grace in accepting a significant if not challenging request — at the witching hour no less — which we are truly grateful for. This willingness has resulted in the very edition you now hold in your hands, reconfigured as it was in the heart of October, long after its initial gestation, & while on the road.

Rainer J. HANSHE

www.ingramcontent.com/pod-product-compliance
Lightning Source LLC
Chambersburg PA
CBHW080544090426
42734CB00016B/3193
9781940625027